THE CAMERA BAG COMPANION

THE CAMERA BAG COMPANION

YOUR PERSONAL PHOTOGRAPHY TUTOR

BENEDICT BRAIN

ilex

Contents

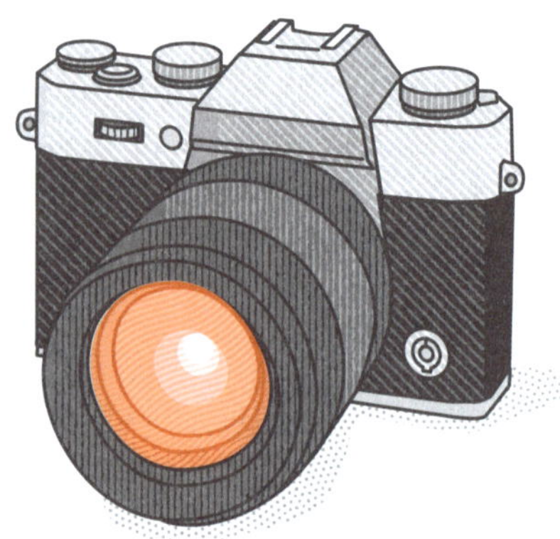

CHAPTER 1
PHOTOGRAPHIC KIT

CHAPTER 2
ESSENTIAL SKILLS

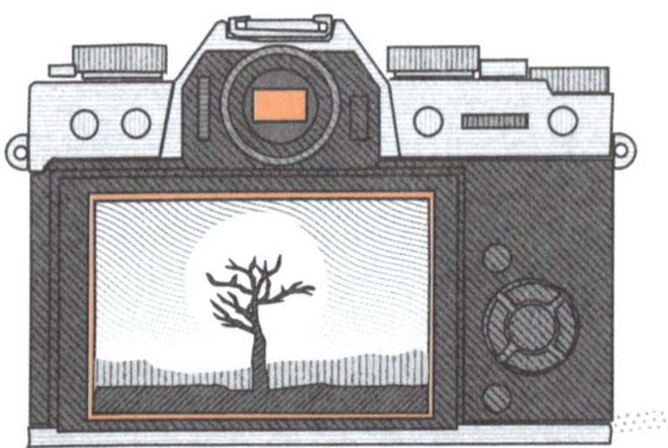

CHAPTER 3
CREATIVE TECHNIQUES

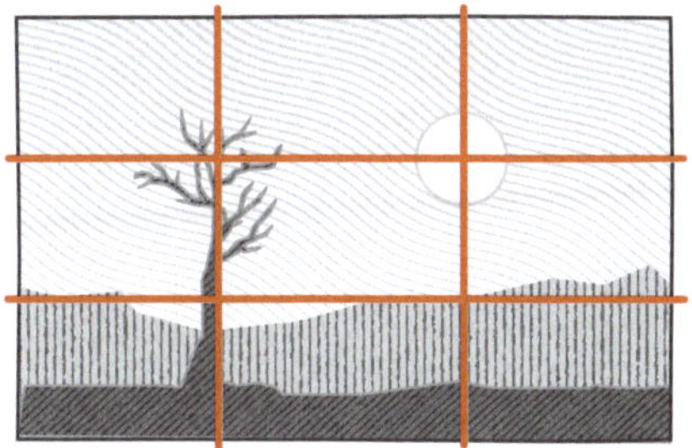

CHAPTER 4
HOW TO PHOTOGRAPH

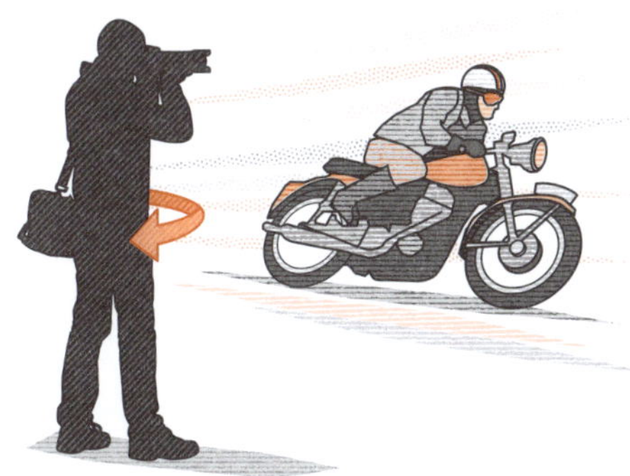

CHAPTER 5
POST-PRODUCTION AND MINDFULNESS

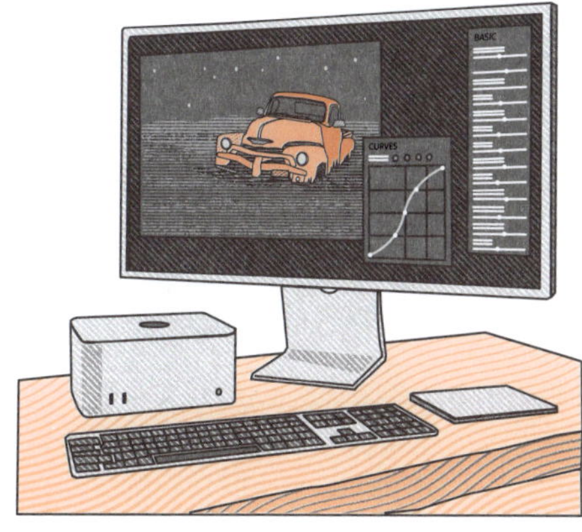

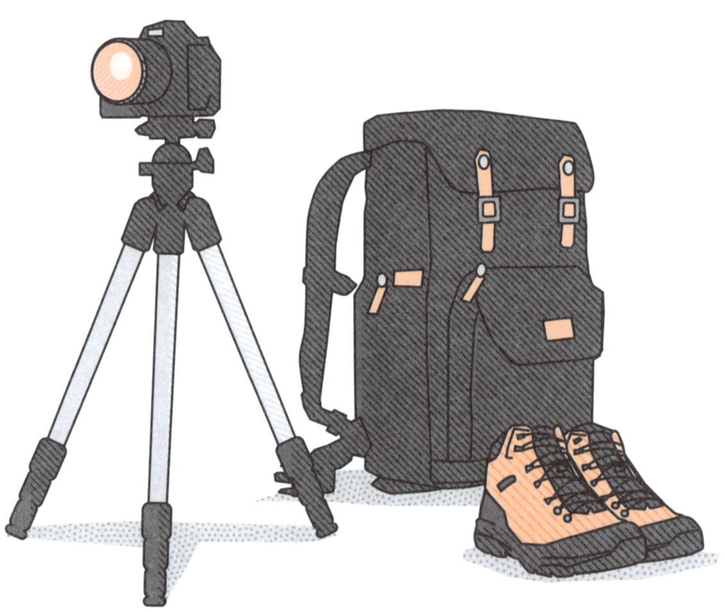

Foreword

Since the early days of photography, there have been many books and general writings covering all the various aspects of what, in my view, is the most wonderfully creative and remarkably exploratory artistic field. When given the right toolset, it is an endeavour that can fully engage and transform all who practise it.

Benedict asks us to acknowledge that our photography should be a process of noticing and discovery; utilizing not only sight but also our hearing, smell, touch and feelings to build an impression before the camera is employed.

Benedict's book offers so much about the crucial importance for the person behind the camera to be assured of producing images that have parity with their own unique creative and human response to the world around them. This is not a book about producing simply a photographic 'record' of a subject.

Be assured that within the accessible pages of this book can be found all the knowledge required to produce photographs that will fulfil the photographer's creative intentions. Designed with ingenious, simple and instantly understandable illustrations, the photographer is guided effortlessly through all the rewarding processes of photography.

This book is from the hand of a photographer who clearly understands all that is needed, both emotionally and technically, to allow you to excel in the wonderful world of photography.

– Charlie Waite
www.charliewaite.com

Introduction

If you're reading this book, the chances are you're feeling ready to take the next steps in your photographic journey. Expressing yourself through the language of photography can be a wonderful thing.

However, there will be a time when to really express yourself, you'll need to take control of your tools, and that means getting to grips with some of the fundamentals of photography.

While smartphone cameras are fabulous tools that make image-making fun and accessible to just about anyone, they can only take you so far and have some limitations. If you're serious about your image-making, understanding the basics of photography along with mastering some essential skills, techniques and theories will give you the creative toolbox you need to take control of your vision and express yourself.

Through a no-nonsense, jargon-free 'conversation', this book will help you explore the fundamentals of photographic theory, giving you a solid foundation for building your photographic practice. Not only will you get to grips with the basics of exposure, camera controls, composition and light, you'll also gain insight into some core creative skills and ideas on how to shoot some of the more popular subjects and genres.

– Benedict Brain
@benedict_brain

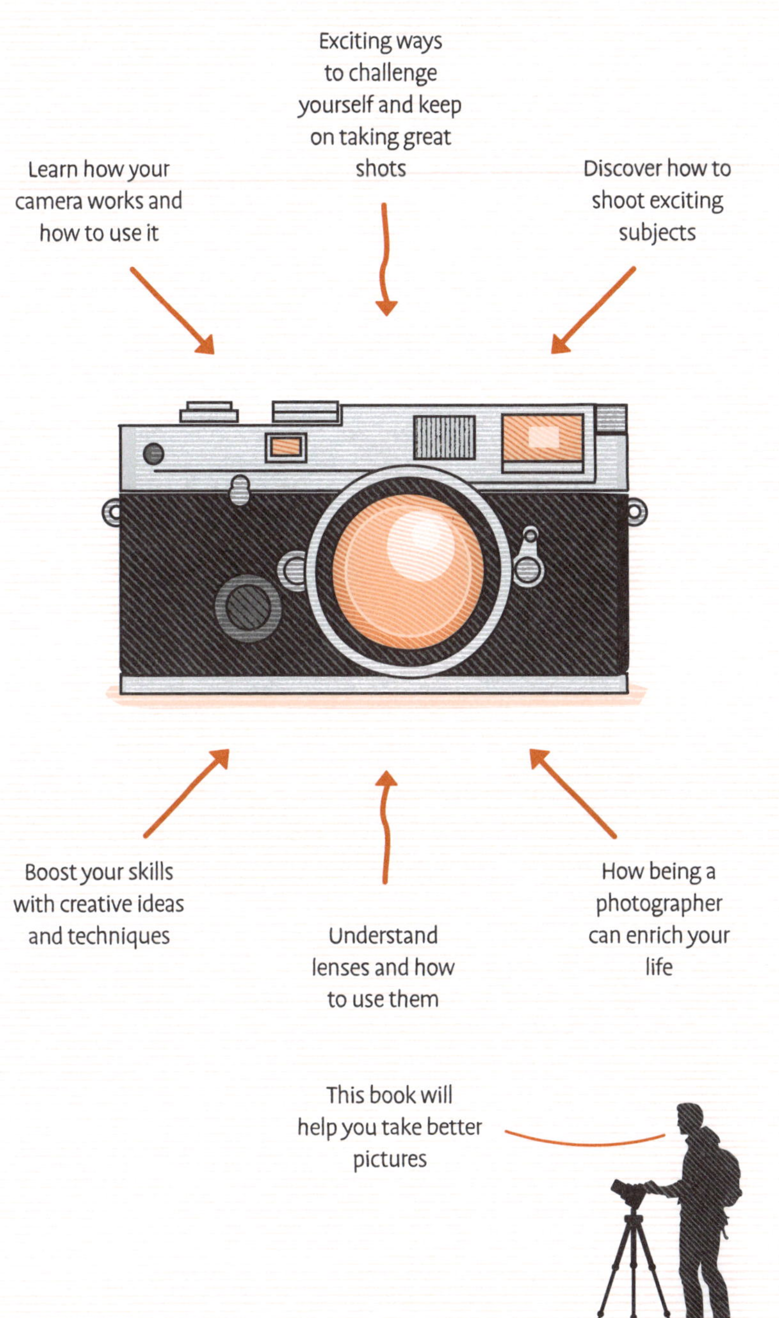
Exciting ways to challenge yourself and keep on taking great shots
Learn how your camera works and how to use it
Discover how to shoot exciting subjects
Boost your skills with creative ideas and techniques
Understand lenses and how to use them
How being a photographer can enrich your life
This book will help you take better pictures

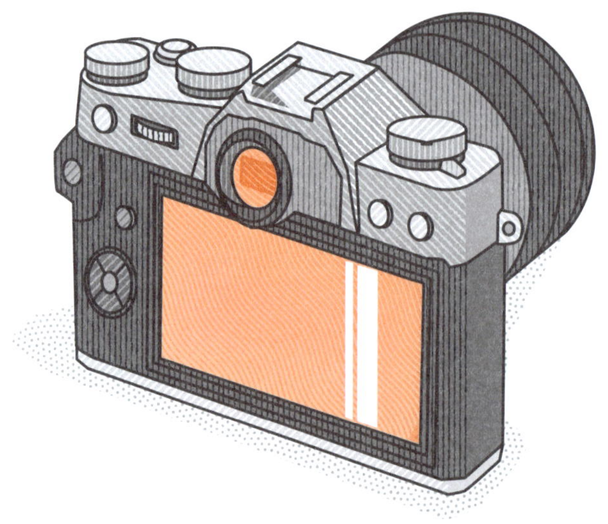

How to use this book

This is a book to keep in your camera bag. The idea is to dip in and out of the book. Keep it on hand as a constant, reassuring and friendly companion on your photographic journey.

You may wonder why there are no photos in a book about photography. Well, the beautiful illustrations tell the story in such a way that it leaves room in your imagination to go in whichever creative direction you like. I don't want you to emulate example photos from a book, I want you to be inspired to find your way of looking and discover your vision and photographic voice.

I want you to feel that through this book, you have a friendly voice close to hand to help, encourage, and point you in the right direction when needed. If you're stuck for creative ideas, use the book as a way to try a new technique or genre that throws you out of your comfort zone. Above all, I want you to use this book to have fun, unleash your creativity and enjoy making photographs unencumbered with boring explanations, technical jargon and overly complicated techniques.

I hope that the book becomes a grubby, dog-eared and much-loved resource for you. You're able to use it as a springboard for further enquiry.

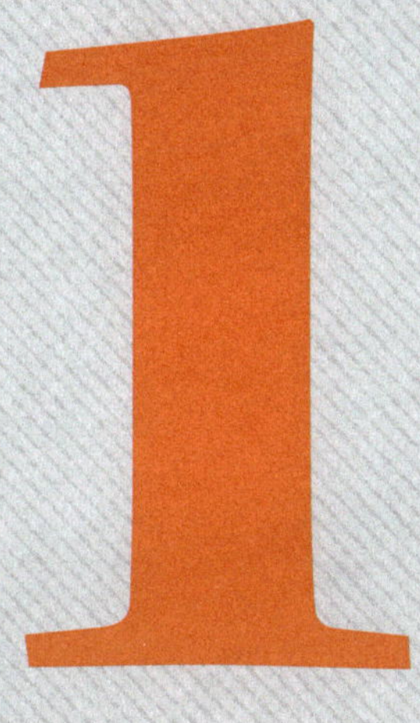

PHOTOGRAPHIC KIT

Camera types

Here's a round up of some of the cameras you're likely to come across on your photographic journey

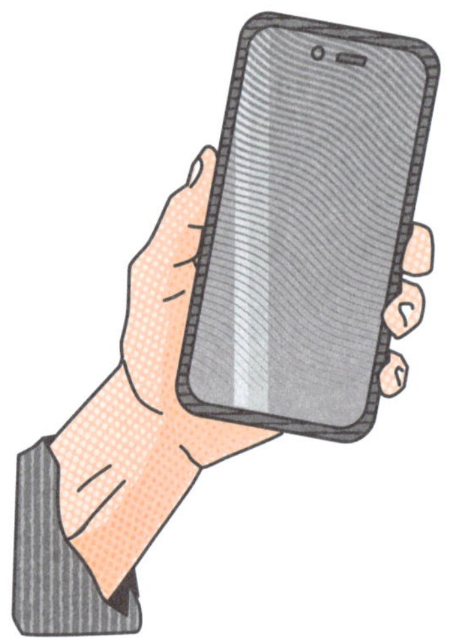

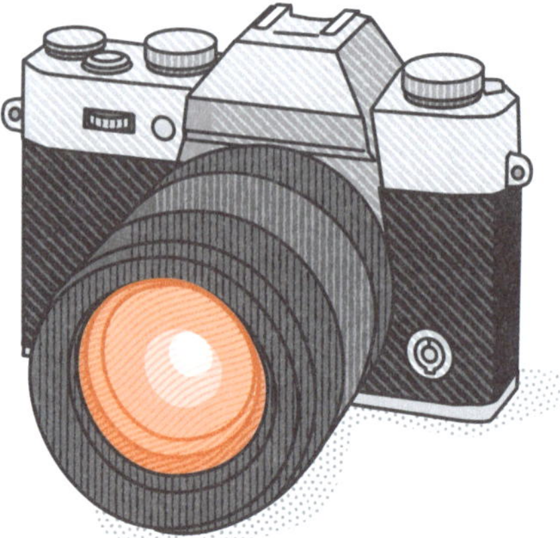

Smartphone
The best camera is the one you've got with you. More often than not, that's your mobile phone's camera. These are generally brilliant, but you have limited control to get creative in the way that you will discover in this book.

DSLR
A conventional single-lens reflex camera (SLR or DSLR) is a standard camera that most people will be familiar with – see overleaf for more.

Mirrorless
A relatively new camera style evolved from DSLRs. See overleaf for more.

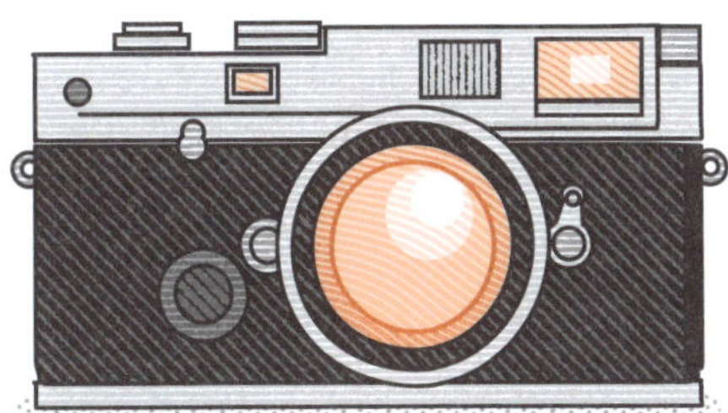

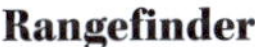

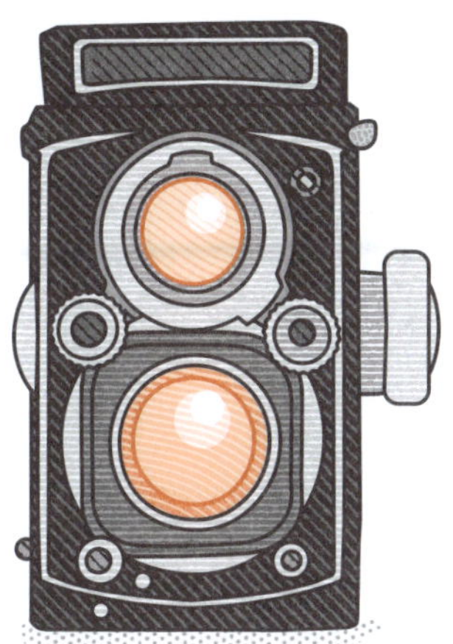

Rangefinder

Rangefinder cameras feature a separate viewfinder, so unlike a DSLR, you won't be looking directly through the lens. The advantage is that the viewfinders are brighter. Rangefinders are typically film cameras, but some digital cameras still use this technology, for example the eye-wateringly expensive Leica M-series cameras.

Medium format

Medium-format cameras simply have larger sensors; they tend to be more specialist and expensive. The larger sensors have a higher resolution, better dynamic range and so on. But unless you have the ambition to make very large fine art prints or are working in advertising, this format will probably be more than you need.

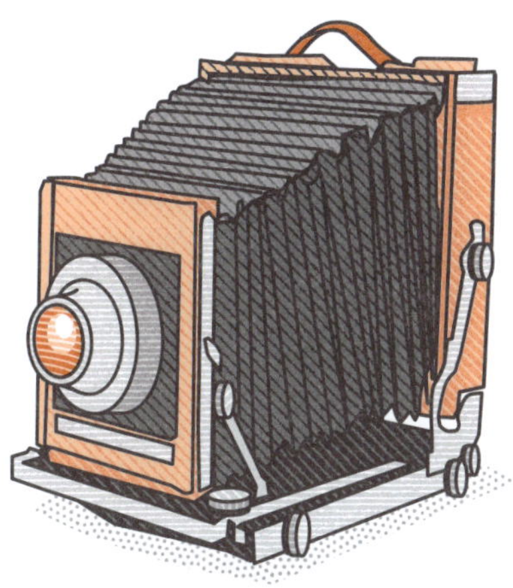

Large format

You can attach film or digital backs to these very technical cameras. The film or sensor area is massive, meaning unparalleled quality. They're also complicated and clunky to use but have the advantage that the lens and film planes can be tilted, shifted and swivelled, giving greater control over planes of focus, converging vertices and so on. This is specialist equipment, not for the faint-hearted and won't be covered in this book.

What is the difference between a mirrorless and a DSLR camera, and which is better?

As you can see from the diagram (opposite), the fundamental difference is in the design. A DSLR has a mirror, and a mirrorless doesn't (obviously). Until relatively recently, DSLRs have been the standard go-to type of camera used by most professionals and serious enthusiasts. However, with technological advances, mirrorless systems have become a more viable option; camera manufacturers seem to be pushing more resources at developing them, and they are becoming more and more popular.

Which should I use?

Both have pros and cons, and you must decide what's important. The main pro of using a DSLR is that the mirror allows you to see through the lens, so you'll see the image exactly as the camera will see it. The way autofocus systems work used to be better on DSLRs. However, advances with mirrorless technology have largely caught up. DSLRs have been around longer than mirrorless cameras, so there is typically a wider range of lenses available, which is a deal-breaker for some people.

By comparison, mirrorless cameras are smaller and more compact, and the range of available lenses is increasing rapidly. It seems that this is the direction camera manufacturers are going. While you may not be looking directly through the lens when using a mirrorless camera, you will look at an electronic rendering of exactly what the camera is seeing, sent to the electronic viewfinder (EVF) or LCD screen directly from the camera's sensor. The quality of this electronic image used to be pretty rubbish, but these days it is generally outstanding. You can also see how the exposure will look and apply any in-camera styles and presets (such as black and white).

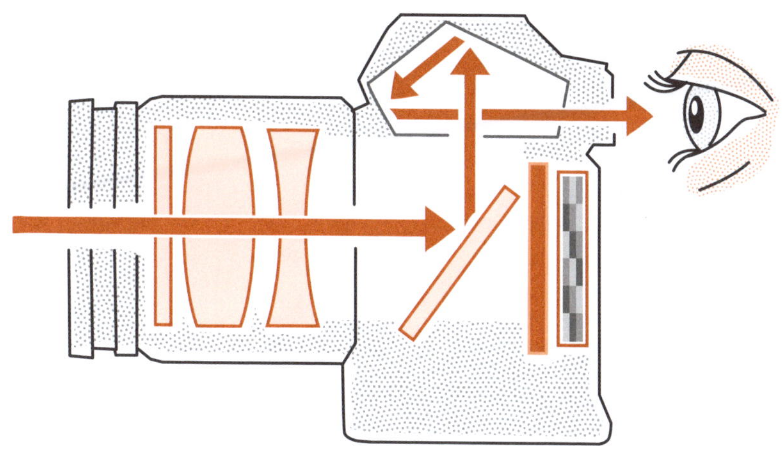

DSLR CAMERA

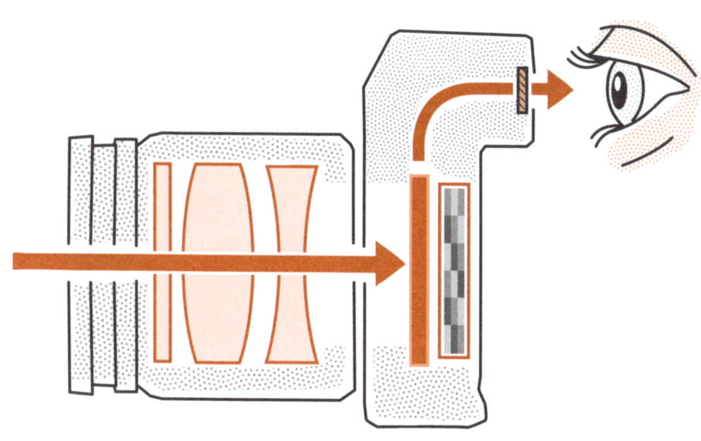

MIRRORLESS CAMERA

Camera basics

What do all the buttons and dials on a camera do?

Each camera is different. However, some features are common to all cameras. The diagram and annotations on these pages will highlight the basics, but you should consult your camera's manual for specifics.

Shutter release

This is what you press to take a photo.

Aperture ring or dial

Use this dial to change the aperture (see page 50). This is sometimes built into the lens and sometimes allocated to a specific dial.

Shutter speed dial

This dial can be used to change the camera's shutter speed.

Mode selection dial

There are a bunch of different shooting modes, from completely manual, where you have control of the camera's settings, to fully automatic or program mode, in which you relinquish control to the camera. We'll discuss all these modes in other parts of the book.

Lens

Seems obvious, right? It is. Remember to remove the cap.

D-pad control

Some cameras have this navigation pad to move focus points around the screen. Not all cameras will have this feature.

LCD screen

The screen on the back of the camera. This is where you can view images that you've taken and where you can access your camera's menu system. It can be difficult to see in bright light.

Viewfinder

You look through this to frame your photo. Increasingly, and especially with mirrorless cameras, this is an electronic viewfinder (EVF), and you'll be looking at a digital image. With a DSLR camera, you'll be looking through the camera's lens.

Focus mode selector

Use this button to switch between manual and autofocus; manual can be helpful in tricky situations such as night photography.

Exposure compensation dial

Use this dial to make your images lighter or darker. Better still, learn the basics of the exposure triangle (see page 40) and adjust your aperture and shutter speed accordingly.

Front command dial

On most cameras the function of this dial can be customized to whatever you wish. I set this to change the ISO, but you may prefer something else.

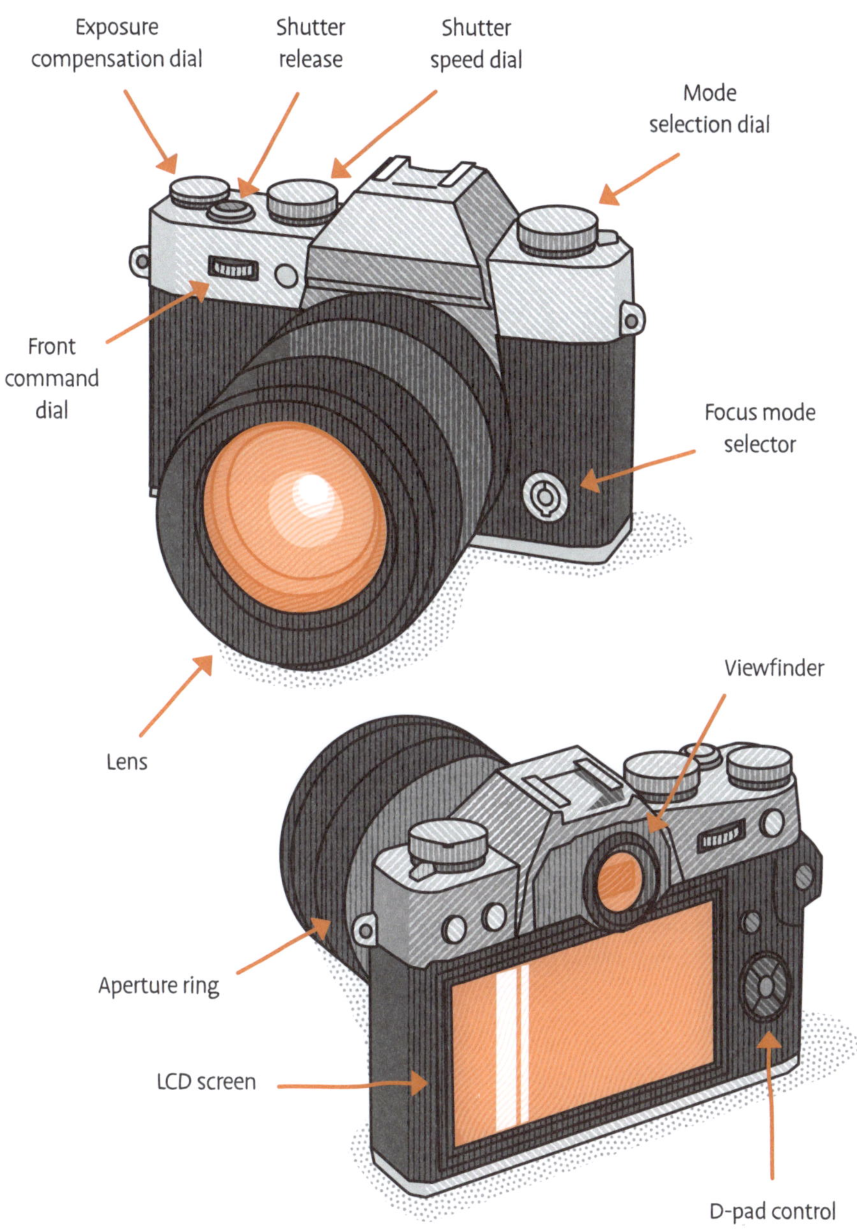
Exposure compensation dial
Shutter release
Shutter speed dial
Mode selection dial
Front command dial
Focus mode selector
Lens
Viewfinder
Aperture ring
LCD screen
D-pad control

The right camera for you

Which camera should I get?

That is a good question and one that is very hard to answer, as it depends on so many varying factors. The first is your budget. In the first instance, be warned, things can start to get expensive quickly, and it's easy to get sucked in by all the marketing, hype and reviews that'll tell you what you need. But even with a level head, have a realistic expectation that there's some investment. It's not just a camera and lenses; you'll need a whole bunch of other equipment, such as memory cards, hard drives and a computer.

My brother uses a Nikon and says that is the way to go. Is he right?

Not really; you should go the way you feel is good for you and your photography. That might be Nikon, but it might not be. You'll no doubt get told that you should do this and that by lots of different people. With the best intentions, their advice can be more confusing than helpful. However, if your brother, friends or family are into photography and have already invested in a system, it could be worth considering using the same system as them, as you may be able to share lenses and accessories, keeping costs down.

What should I look for?

You should ask yourself first what you think you will most likely want to photograph. Most modern cameras boast many features and functions, but honestly, many won't make you a better photographer, and in many cases, they'll be wasted on you. For example, if you are passionate about creating slow, mindfully considered landscapes, why would you need a camera that can shoot 13 frames per second? You probably wouldn't, so it's not worth paying for it. Look for a camera that's more suited to what you need. That might be a high-resolution sensor so you can make large prints or capture more detail for landscape photography, or it might be super-fast focusing and 12 frames per second for action and wildlife.

A camera is just a creative tool; it is important to choose the right tool and that you can understand how to use it easily. If you can, take the time to go to a camera store and get a sense of how it feels to use. Even a half-decent camera store should be able to help you navigate the complexities and, at the very least, let you hold one and get a feel for it. Events like the Photography Show in the UK are great places to test gear, and many countries host similar events.

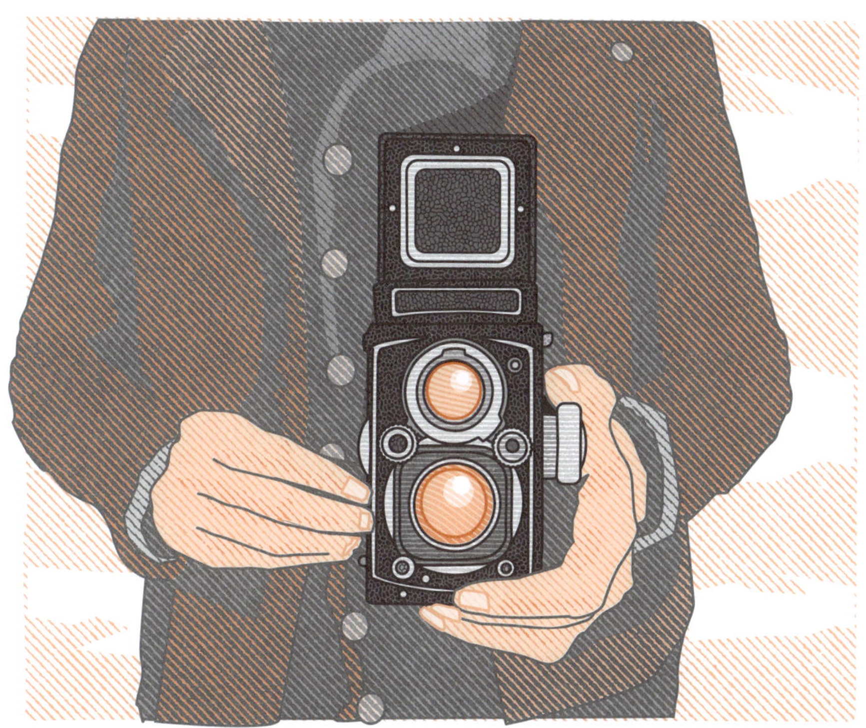

What about a secondhand camera?
Great question! There are some excellent deals on used equipment, and it's a sensible option to consider, especially if you're on a budget. However, like anything secondhand, there's a risk involved. Some reputable online companies even offer a warranty that gives you peace of mind.

How light is captured

How does a sensor work?
Very crudely and in a sentence or two, a camera's sensor comprises millions of photodiodes (pixels) that capture light. When you press the shutter release, the sensor is exposed to light, effectively opening the door to let the light in. The photodiodes convert light into an electrical charge which is in turn converted into digital values, and an image is formed.

Why do sensors come in different sizes?
The sensor size refers to the physical dimensions of the image sensor in your digital camera. Different sensor sizes impact image quality and camera performance. What you choose depends on many factors, but most significantly, your budget, what you intend to photograph and what you plan to do with the photographs.

Based on the size and ratio of a 35mm film frame (36x24mm), full-frame sensors have high image quality, wide dynamic range and good low-light performance. APS-C sensors (typically around 22x15mm) are smaller, resulting in a narrower field of view and minor image-quality differences. Micro Four Thirds sensors (17.3x13mm) are even smaller, offering portability and a deep depth of field, although it's harder to achieve a shallow depth of field.

Smaller sensors like those found in smartphones are tiny by comparison, so the image quality and ability to achieve a shallow depth of field is limited. However, as we all know, they offer convenience and portability. Even medium- and large-format sensors exist and offer unparalleled image quality and the ability to achieve a super-shallow depth of field, but these are also very expensive.

What's the difference between sensor types?
There are several types of image sensors: CCD (charge-coupled device) sensors and CMOS (complementary metal-oxide-semiconductor) are the main ones available in consumer cameras. CCD sensors offer high image quality but consume more power. CMOS sensors are more widely used due to their low power consumption and versatility. Sigma Imaging makes a Foveon sensor, which captures light differently and has the potential to be interesting but is quite niche.

ANATOMY OF A CAMERA SENSOR

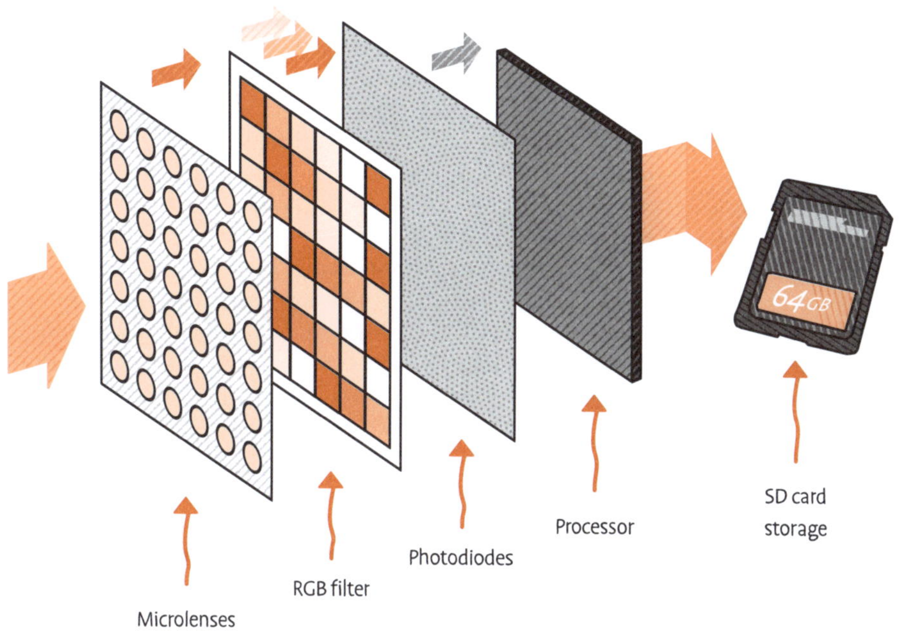

Lenses

One of the advantages of DSLR and mirrorless cameras is the ability to change lenses. However, deciding which lens to use presents a minefield of choices that can be quite confusing and expensive.

Where should I start?

Many photographers argue, and I agree, that you're better off spending your money on decent glass than fancy cameras. Start simply and build from that. Typically, the 'kit' lenses that come with entry-level cameras are not great, but they'll be fine to get you going. However, you'll no doubt want to tease out more quality from your glass in time. Think about starting with one simple prime lens.

Okay, which lens would you start with?

A 50mm lens is generally considered a 'standard' lens; some even call it 'the nifty fifty'. Its field of view is not far from the human eye, so it'll feel natural to use. Start with this and just use one lens for a year or so. It will make you a better photographer, guaranteed.

What about other focal lengths?

There's a whole bunch, from extremely wide-angle to telephoto, as shown in the diagram. Selecting the right focal length to work with is an essential part of the creative process. Not only are there a lot of focal lengths to choose from, there are other considerations too, which we'll look at over the next couple of pages.

Why do people mention 35mm equivalent when talking about lenses?

The term '35mm' has become a standard way of measuring, comparing and getting a sense of a lens's field of view. It's based on how a lens's angle of view would appear when using a traditional 35mm film camera; the size of the 35mm film is also the same as a full-frame sensor and has become a standard. So, to have a similar field of view as a 50mm lens on a full-frame (35mm) camera, you would typically need a lens with a focal length of around 35mm on an APS-C camera. The smaller APS-C sensors have a 'crop factor', often around 1.5x or 1.6x, effectively increasing the focal length. So, a lens with a focal length of approximately 35mm on an APS-C sensor would provide a similar field of view as a 50mm lens on a full-frame camera.

LENSES – FIELD OF VIEW

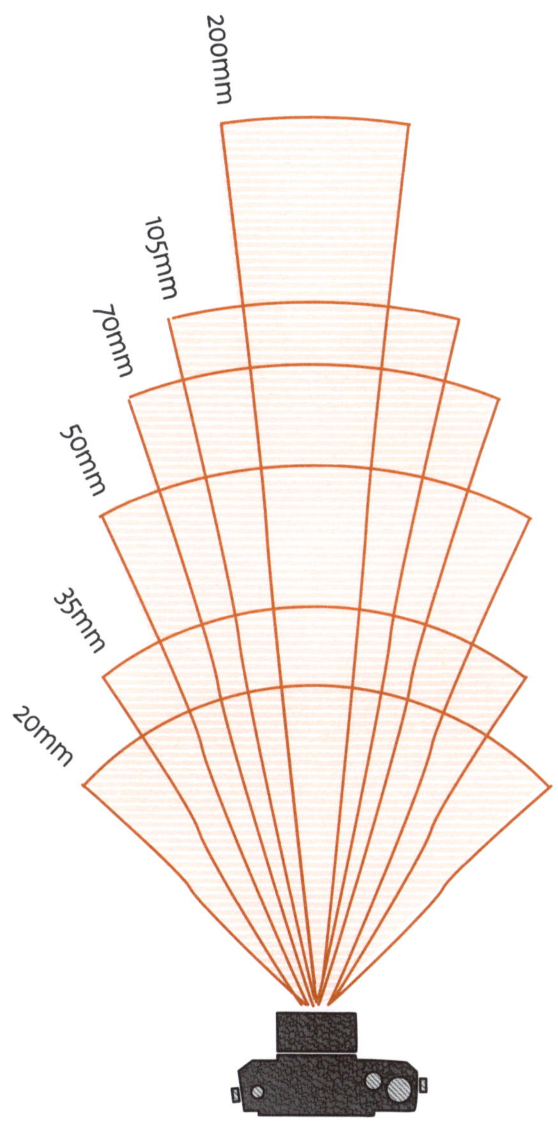

How does a lens work?

Put simply, a lens is a transparent optical element, usually glass, that focuses light onto a camera's image sensor. It works by bending light rays as they pass through it. Convex lenses converge incoming parallel rays of light, while concave lenses diverge them. This bending of light allows the lens to control the direction and focus of the light rays, forming a sharp and clear image on the camera's sensor. The lens's shape determines its focal length, affecting the magnification. A typical camera lens is made by moulding glass into specific shapes. The glass is then ground and polished to refine its surface. Various coatings, such as anti-reflective, are added, and the elements, of which there are typically many, are assembled into a lens barrel with rings for focus and aperture control.

How does image stabilization work?

Some lenses have a switch on the lens barrel to turn image stabilization on or off. It cleverly uses gyroscopic sensors and moving lens elements to keep things steady and help you get sharper shots.

Why would I ever turn it off?

Switching it off when using a tripod is advisable, as the motors might cause some vibration. Also if you're using panning techniques to photograph sports and action shots (see page 146).

Is it worth having?

Yes, especially with big and heavy telephoto or zoom lenses. It can save you from reaching for the tripod, cranking up your ISO or using artificial light.

HOW A LENS WORKS

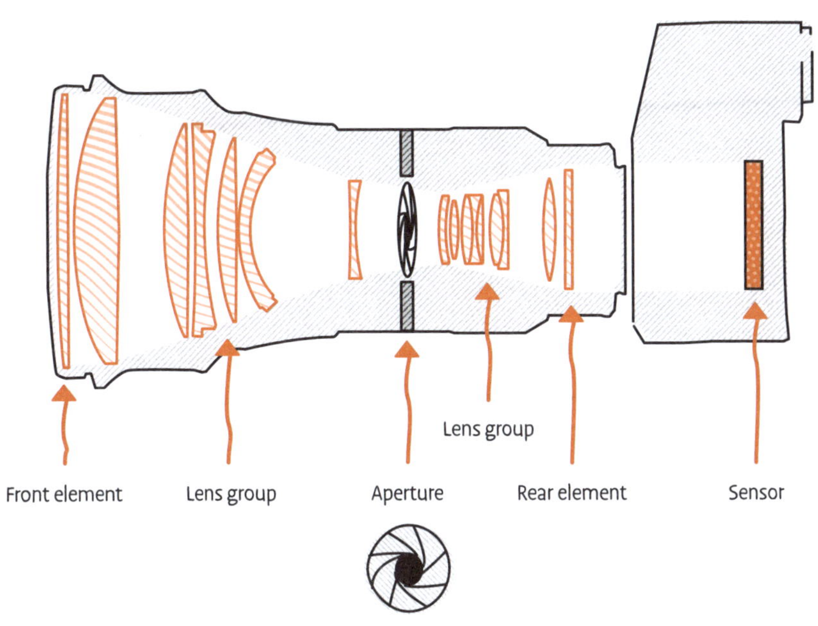

WIDE-ANGLE LENS

TELEPHOTO LENS

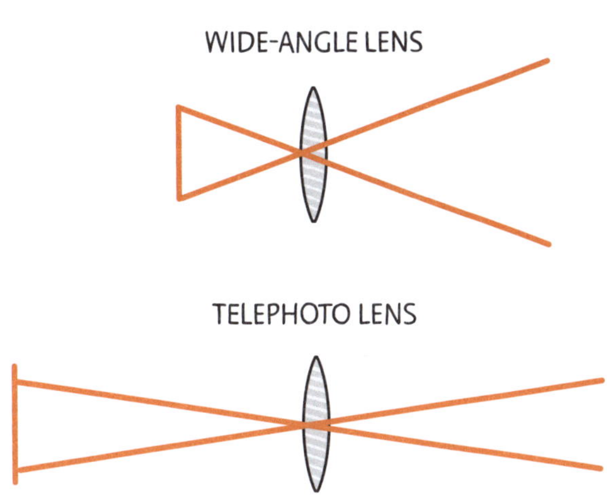

What is a prime lens?

Unlike a zoom lens with a variable range of focal lengths, a prime lens has one fixed focal length. You'll need to physically move if you want your subject to be further away or closer, or switch to another prime. The upside is that primes are typically, but not always, better-quality lenses. There is less compromise in the design and construction of a prime, so the optical quality is worth the restriction. On the flip side, if you want a decent range of focal lengths, you may carry around a whole bunch of heavy glass. Also, changing lenses on location can expose your super-sensitive and vulnerable sensor to the elements, running the risk of dust and dirt getting into your camera.

Why would I bother with carrying a whole bunch of primes lenses when I could just use one zoom lens?

Most photographers prefer to work with zoom lenses, although it's worth noting that zoom lenses don't typically cover the whole range of focal lengths. For example, you'll find wide-angle zooms normally ranging from 20–35mm, mid-range zooms from 24–70mm and telephoto zooms from 70–200mm. You won't find one from 14–600mm. Some have a more comprehensive range than others, but as a general rule, the wider the range, the more the image quality is compromised. Also, zooms are often bigger, bulkier and heavier.

What's a macro lens?

A macro lens allows you to focus very close to your subject and is typically used by nature photographers wanting to capture insects and plants, along with medical and forensic photographers. Macro lenses come in a range of focal lengths. For more on close-up photography and using a macro lens, see page 138.

And what about a tilt-shift lens?

A tilt-shift lens is a specialist lens that allows you to selectively focus and control perspective by tilting and shifting the lens elements. Professional architectural and interior photographers typically use them for perspective control and advertising, and landscape photographers for focus control. For more on using a tilt-shift lens, turn to page 96.

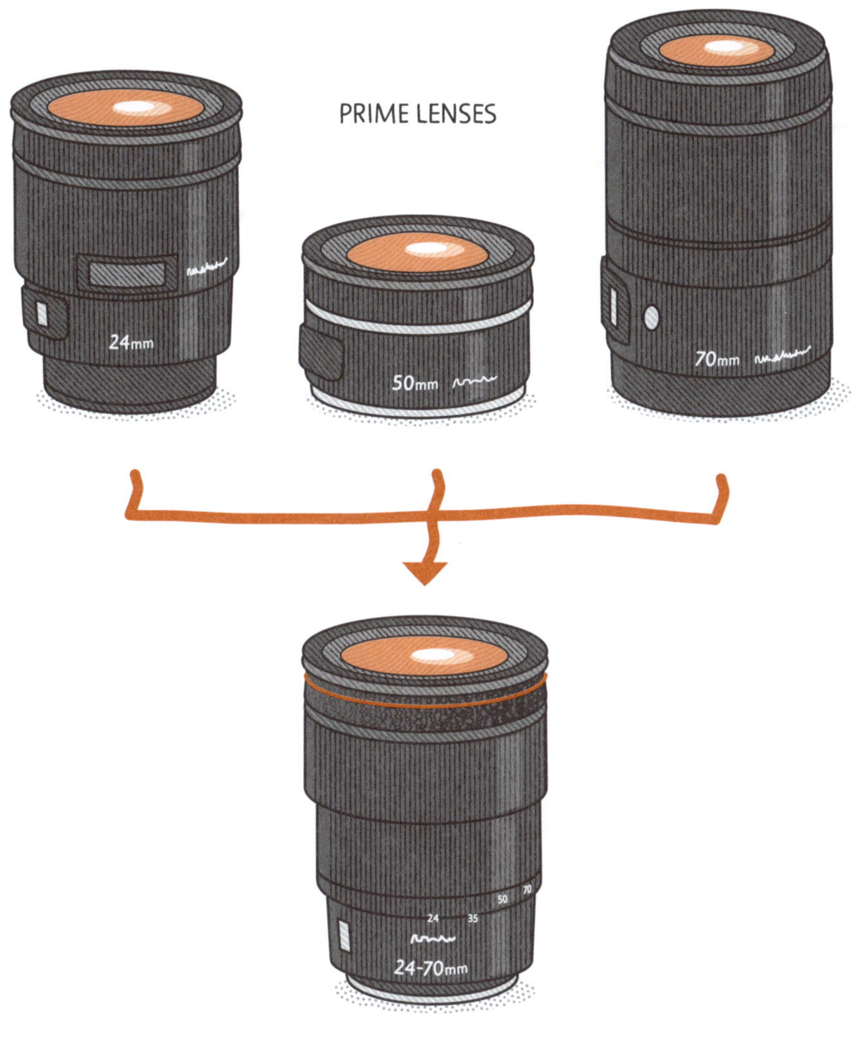
PRIME LENSES
24mm
50mm
70mm
50
70
24
35
24-70mm
ZOOM LENS

What's a 'fast' lens?

'Fast' is a term that's attributed to lenses with a wide maximum aperture. Typically, this is f/2.8 or wider (f/1.4). 'Fast' implies that faster shutter speeds can be used. In low-light conditions, this has a massive advantage, and they are consequently desirable with photographers working in these conditions, such as street, documentary and sports photographers. However, there are other benefits to a wide maximum aperture, such as the ability to achieve a greater depth of field (see page 50), so they are also extremely popular with portrait photographers. Fast lenses are more expensive than regular lenses, mainly due to the use of superior optics and the technical complexities of production. This is why a 50mm f/1.4 lens costs significantly more than a 50mm f/5.6 lens.

Why does my zoom lens have two widest apertures?

Some zoom lenses have a constant maximum aperture throughout the range of focal lengths. However, most zoom lenses indicate two widest apertures. Widest apertures are often available at the lens's shortest focal length, while the maximum aperture decreases as you zoom in. It's another option to consider when weighing up your budget and what you want to photograph.

What about bokeh?

Bokeh is another reason why photographers are attracted to wide-aperture lenses. Bokeh is a term used to describe the aesthetic quality of the out-of-focus parts of an image. This quality is more evident if you're shooting with wide apertures, such as f/2.8. The configuration, shape and number of aperture blades in the lens, along with the quality of the glass used, all have an impact on the characteristics of a lens's bokeh. Sometimes, technically flawed lenses reveal a beautiful bokeh which, while imperfect, can become highly coveted. Look at your lens and see what the bokeh looks like and how different apertures affect it. When you're composing your images, it's easy to focus your attention on the main, usually sharply focused, subject, but be mindful of the blurred parts too, as these can be just as important.

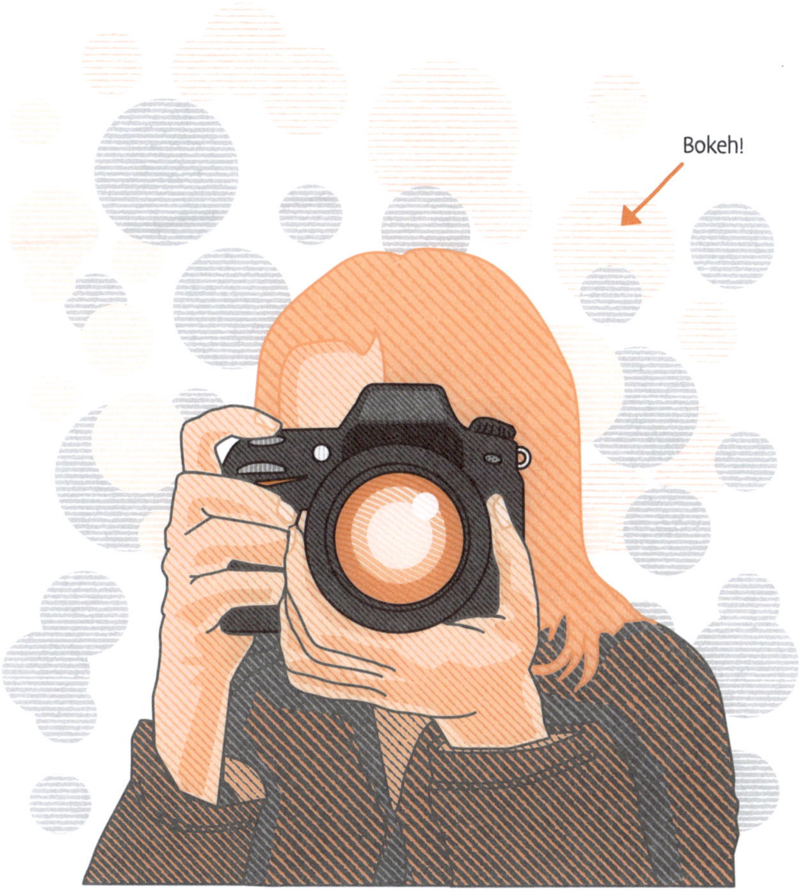

Bokeh!

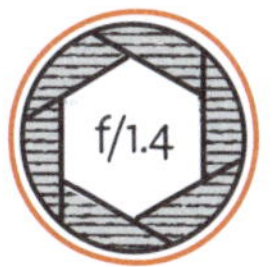

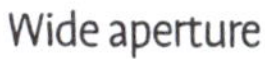
Wide aperture

Fast lens

Accessories

In addition to your camera and at least one lens, you're going to need a few accessories. Annoyingly, photography can be quite an expensive endeavour. It's worth it, though.

A tripod

A tripod is not essential for all types of photography, such as street photography. However, it's a helpful tool to help you in low-light situations, especially when slow shutter speeds are involved. In a nutshell, it keeps your camera steady. Tripods come in all shapes and sizes and a wide range of prices. You'll also be able to choose the type of tripod 'head' (the bit you attach your camera to), such as a ball-and-socket head or a three-way head; it's just down to personal preference. Try them out and see what works for you. A monopod is another option that some photographers, especially sports and wildlife photographers, like. A monopod only has one leg (obviously), so it won't keep a camera perfectly still, but it will help take the weight of big, heavy telephoto lenses.

Backpack or shoulder bag

A decent shoulder bag or backpack to carry your accessories, spare lenses, batteries, memory cards, snacks, water, and so on is a good idea. A shoulder bag has the benefit of being quick and easy to access, but not so good on the shoulders. Backpacks, however, are great for long hikes but difficult to access and can tempt you to take more than you need. Whatever you choose, keep it small and travel light.

Remote trigger

Plug this into your camera so you don't have to touch it during a long exposure. This will help avoid unwanted camera movement (see page 46–7), which can be caused by the act of pressing the shutter release. You can use your camera's self-timer if you don't have one. A lot of camera manufacturers have an associated app to accompany their kit; these apps often include a remote trigger, typically via a Wi-Fi or Bluetooth connection. Some are better than others.

SD cards and case

It's always good to carry spare memory cards. Carry them in a special case to help protect them from bumps, knocks and water. Memory cards are sensitive little things, so you must look after them. They come in different capacities and 'write speeds' and choosing which ones to purchase largely depends on what you photograph. Always format your cards in the camera before starting a new shoot – consult your camera's manual to find out how.

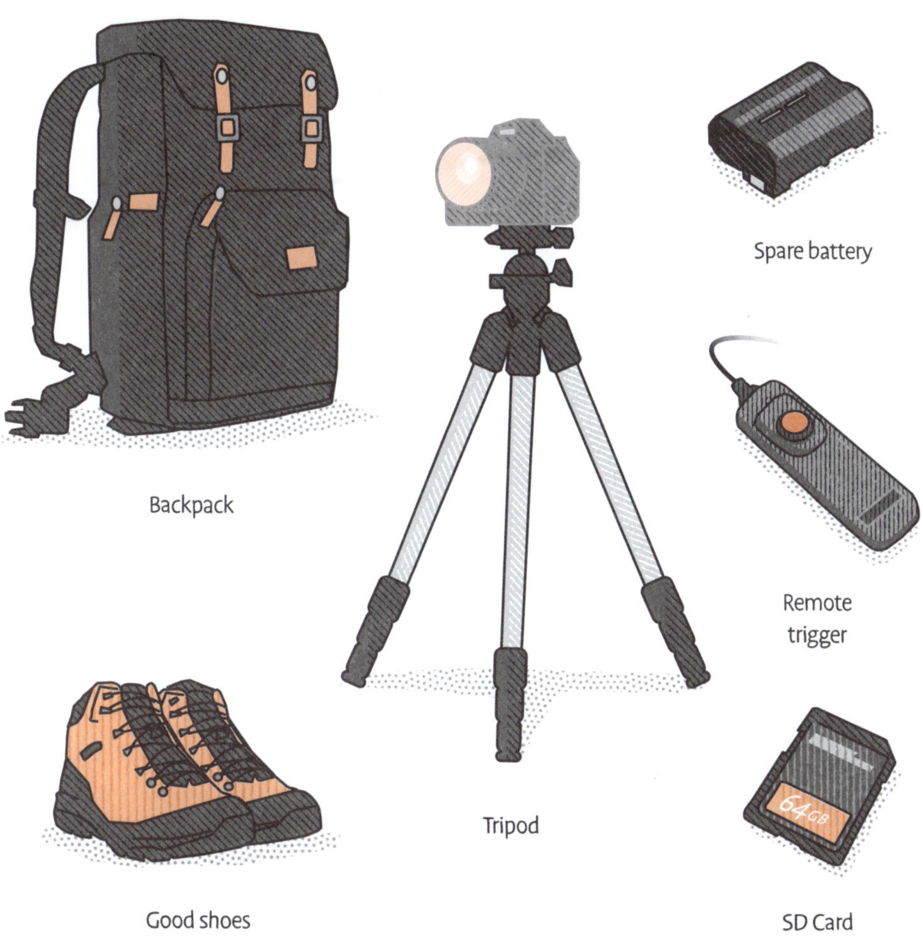

Spare batteries
Digital cameras, with their power-hungry sensors, LCDs and so on, can burn through batteries quickly, especially if it's cold. You'll likely need a spare (or two) and double-check that everything is fully charged before heading out.

Good shoes
Decent footwear and appropriate clothing are vital. There's nothing more likely to inhibit the creative process than being cold and wet with sore, blistered feet. There is no such thing as bad weather, just bad clothing, as they say.

Filters

These days, very few effects cannot be emulated with image-editing software. This means photographers don't need to carry around as many optical filters as they used to. However, some effects still require a filter; depending on what you want to photograph, you may want to add them to your camera bag.

Neutral-density filter
A neutral-density filter (ND) is like a pair of sunglasses. You place it over your lens, preventing light from getting in.

Why would you want to do this?
These filters are usually used for long-exposure photography. ND filters typically come in densities of 3, 5 and 10 stops. So, for example, if your exposure is f/11 at 1/125sec, ISO 100, but you want a slower shutter speed, add a 5-stop ND filter, keep your aperture and ISO the same, and increase the amount of time your shutter is open by 5 stops (which would be 1/4sec) to achieve the same exposure value. If you want more blur, use a higher ND filter.

Graduated neutral-density filter
These are a bit like ND filters, only they feature a transition from clear to dark (you can easily see this transition when you hold them up to the light). Like ND filters, they come in various densities. However, they also come with varying degrees of transition – some have hard transitions while others have soft transitions. ND grads typically come in sets and are most often used by landscape photographers who battle with the brightness of the sky compared with the darkness of the land and their camera's limited dynamic range. It's essentially a way of balancing the exposure of the sky and the land so they're more evenly exposed.

Why are they rectangular and not round like other filters?
Round filters that screw onto the front of the lens are fine in many circumstances, but with ND grads in particular, you may want to change where the transition line is so it relates to where you've positioned the horizon line in your composition. Having a square or rectangular filter enables you to move the filter up and down to align it accordingly.

What if a tree or mountain is poking into the sky?
Then you've got a challenge, as the tree or mountain will start to get darker along with the sky. You'll probably be able to save it at the image-editing stage, but it's also a situation where you might use a softer-transition ND filter rather than a hard one.

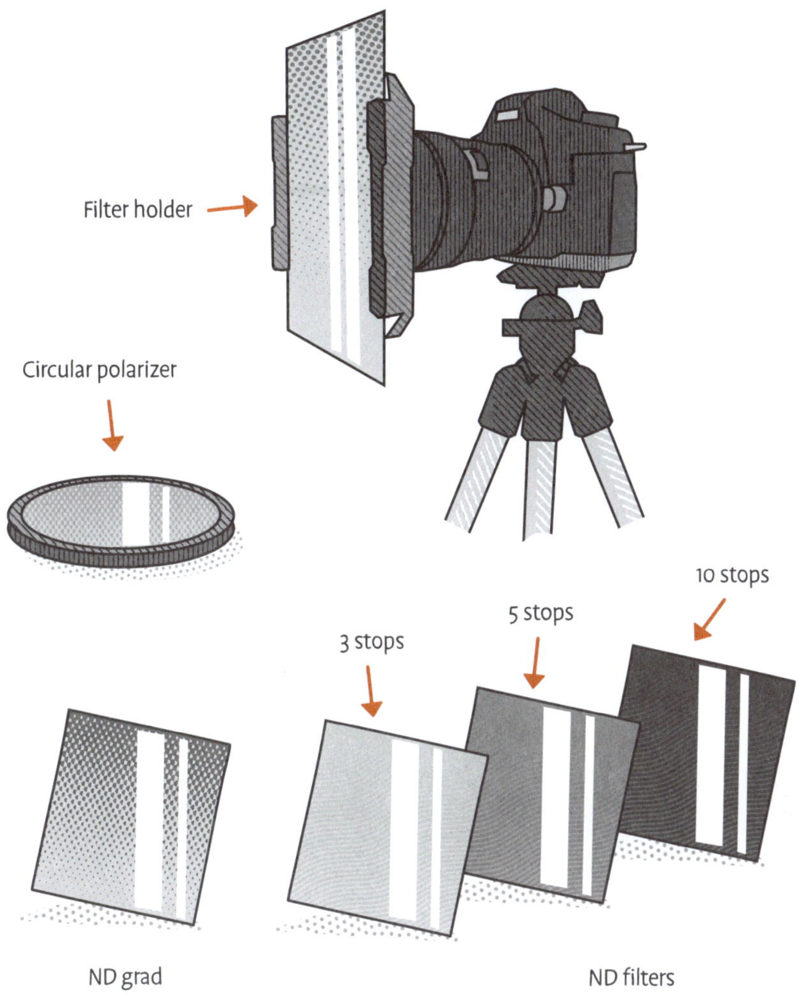

A circular polarizing filter
A circular polarizer reduces glare and reflections, enhances colour saturation and increases the contrast in photographs. It's a popular filter with 'classic' landscape photographers. The filter comprises two pieces of glass that must be rotated to get results. You can see the effect clearly through the viewfinder, so it's intuitive.

Ultraviolet (UV) filter
A UV filter blocks ultraviolet light and can help eliminate the bluish haze in some landscape situations. Most photographers just use them to protect their lenses from dust and scratches.

Photographic kit: Recap

There's no avoiding the fact that photography requires a bunch of technical kit. The relatively complex tools can be costly, and there are myriad options to choose from. On top of that, there's no doubt that everyone you ask will give you different advice on what's best. At the end of the day, making a good photograph is much more down to the skill and vision of the photographer than the equipment they use. However, choosing the right kit is a vital part of the process.

Five top tips

1 Consider the kind of photography you want to make and research what kit other photographers working in that field are using.

2 Keep it simple: all the bells and whistles in the world won't make you a better photographer, and neither will the most expensive kit.

3 Take the time to understand how your camera works. Ultimately, you want to be able to visualize the world the way your camera will see it.

4 Use one lens with a fixed focal length (such as 50mm or 35mm). I guarantee it will make you a better photographer, even if you have to walk to make things appear closer or farther away.

5 The best camera is the one that's with you; more often than not that'll be your smartphone. Embrace this fact – they're great tools.

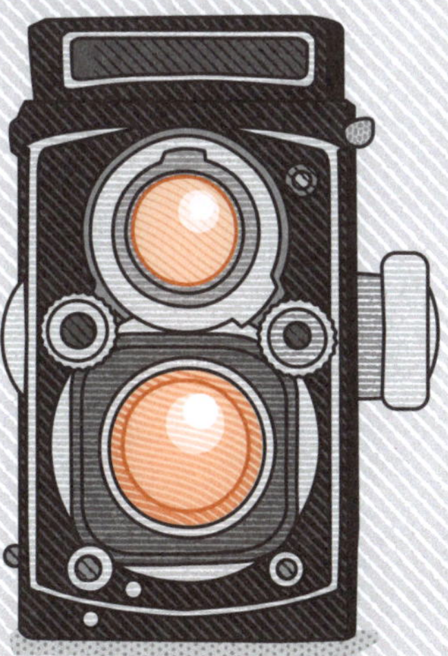

2

ESSENTIAL SKILLS

Exposure basics

The exposure triangle

In terms of understanding the basic principles of photography, these two pages are arguably the most important in the whole book. They're not creatively exciting but take the time to understand the exposure triangle and the relationship between aperture, shutter speed and ISO, and you'll unlock the door to endless creative possibilities without being told what to do by a camera.

Tell me more about the 'exposure triangle' and how I get started...

First, switch your camera to manual mode so that you have complete control over aperture, shutter speed and ISO. In the first instance, try and make a good exposure – you can use the histogram (see overleaf) to help with this. Aim to make an exposure with a good range of tones. Now, experiment by changing the settings (keep your ISO the same, as this has the most negligible impact on your image's appearance).

Notice that if you make the aperture smaller by jumping from, say, f/8 to f/16, the picture gets darker. This is because less light can get through the smaller hole. So, what do you do? You let less light in, but for a longer duration, so if you've prevented 2 stops of light from entering the lens by making the aperture smaller, you need to let 2 stops of light in by increasing the amount of time the shutter is open for, so that could be a jump from 1/250sec to 1/60sec. This is because 1/250sec at f/8 has the same exposure value as 1/60sec at f/16, so in terms of tonality, they will both look the same.

However, the characteristics of the image will alter, as the smaller aperture (f/16) will affect the depth of field (explained on page 50) and so the image will appear sharper than at f/8.

That's insane!

It is! But there's no shortcut – the best way is to practise, experiment and practise some more. It's like a juggling act and we'll look at the effect of shutter speed, ISO and aperture over the next couple of pages. But keep the exposure triangle in mind when considering exposure. Take the time to understand the relationship between the elements and their effect on the image to the extent that it's intuitive, and you'll be on your way.

THE EXPOSURE TRIANGLE

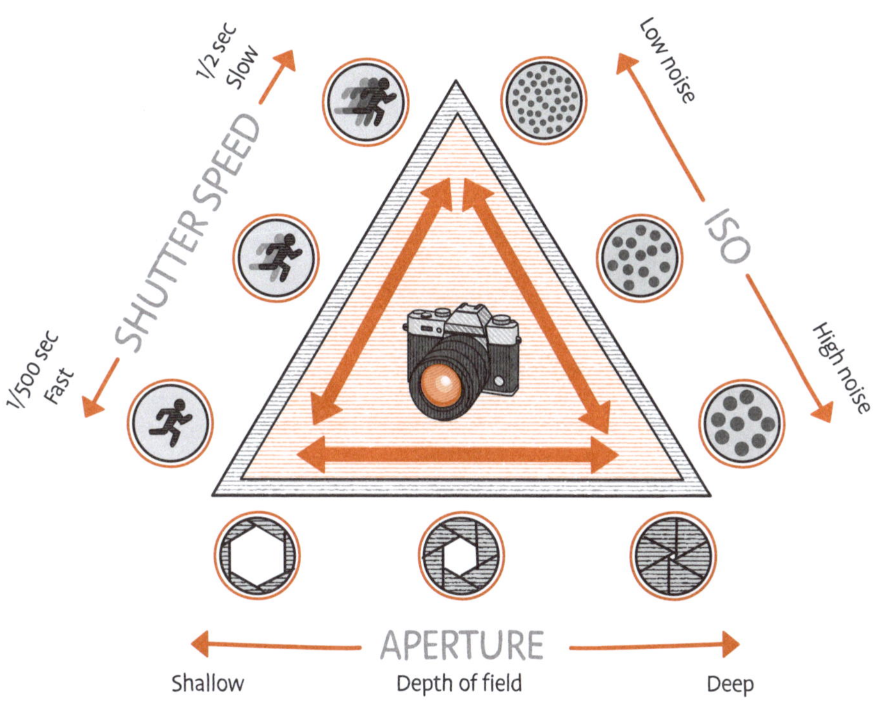

What is a histogram? It sounds scary.
You're right, it does sound scary, but it's not as complicated to understand as most people think. And once you get your head around it, it's a useful tool to help you with exposure.

How can I use this in practice, and why should I bother?
Most modern digital cameras feature a display mode that enables a histogram view of your image, more often as an overlay. You can use the histogram to see a graphical representation of the tones in your photo. This is much more accurate than the image you typically see on the screen, which can sometimes be wildly different from the data captured by your camera. It's especially useful in determining if highlights have been 'clipped' or not.

What's a 'clipped' highlight?
This area of the image is so light or overexposed it has no detail at all; the tonal value has effectively gone off the edge of the right-hand side of the histogram graph and no amount of post-processing wizardry will be able to retrieve detail. Sometimes, it's fine to have areas that are completely overexposed ('blown') – specular highlights, for example, don't need detail. However, it's generally good practice to have some detail in the lightest parts of an image, such as the sky. Using the histogram helps you 'see' this more accurately than the image on the screen.

What about highlight clipping alerts?
Many cameras have a feature that will alert you to 'blown' highlights. Typically, the blown area will flash. This can be very useful.

THE HISTOGRAM

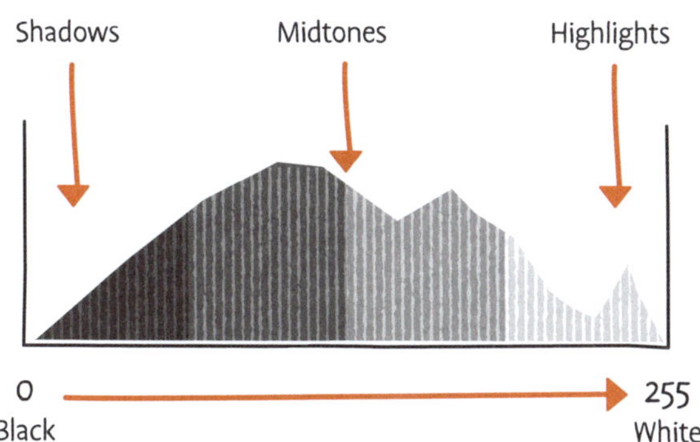

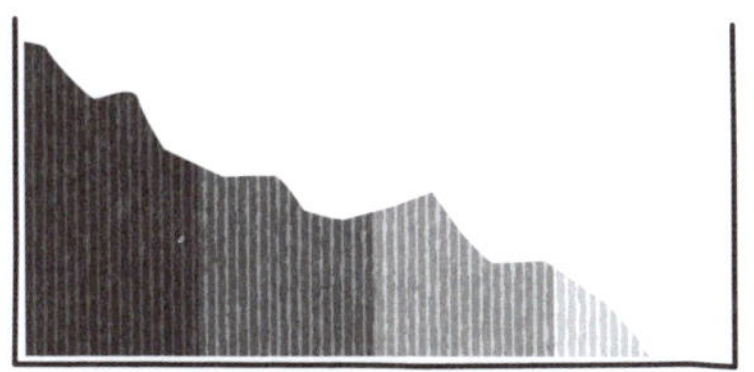

Dark image with 'clipped' blacks

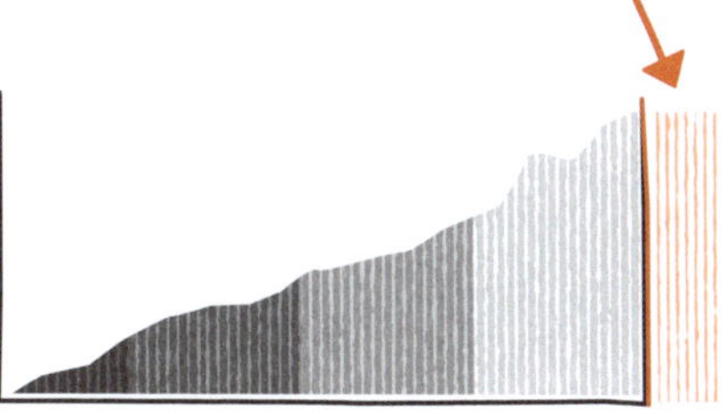

Light image with 'clipped' highlights

What are all the exposure modes and which one should I use?

All cameras will measure (meter) the light entering the camera and calculate the best exposure. However, the camera has zero creativity and, crudely put, wants to make everything mid-tone grey. Given half a chance, it'll turn something black to grey and likewise something white, which is why you must compensate when shooting in snow, for example.

There are a variety of metering modes, matrix (sometimes called evaluative or multi), centre-weighted and spot being the most common. You can set which one to use, giving you varying degrees of control over exposure. Matrix metering is the most common, and in this mode, the scene is divided into measured segments from which an average 'good' exposure is determined. Centre-weighted metering works on the same principle, but the exposure is biased to read the central part of a scene. And spot metering does what you might expect and 'reads' the light from a very small, focused area. There's no right or wrong mode to select, but knowing which one you're using and when to change is important.

When should I use exposure compensation?

Most cameras feature an exposure compensation dial or button. This lets you tell the camera that you want it to be darker or lighter than it says the scene should be. Snow is a good example, and typically to maintain its whiteness so it doesn't become a muddy grey, you need to dial in 2 stops of overexposure, which will make it lighter. Some photographers prefer to ignore this and simply use manual mode. It doesn't matter what you do, but it is useful to understand why.

THE MODE DIAL

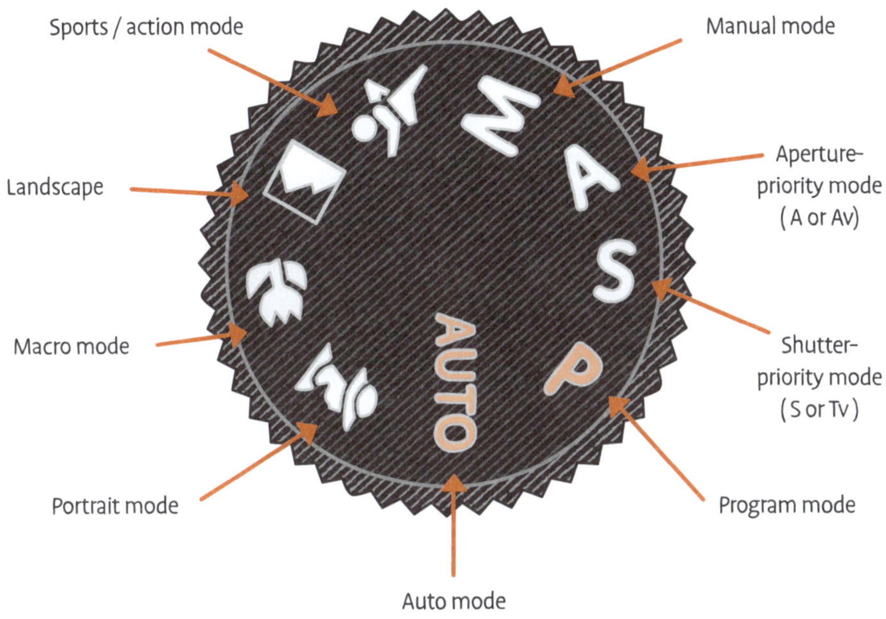

Shutter speed

Let's discuss your camera's shutter, as it's a vital part of the exposure triangle. The shutter is like a gate that opens and closes, letting light into the camera for a short period of time, typically fractions of a second. How long or short it is open for can have a big effect on how your image will look.

What's the best way to control the shutter?
To take a picture, you simply press the shutter button, typically on the top right-hand side of a camera. Use your index finger to gently squeeze rather than jab the shutter button.

Use the shutter speed dial or button to change the speed. In full manual mode, it's a case of selecting your desired shutter speed. In the program and fully automatic modes, your camera will simply select the most suitable shutter speed for a 'good' exposure. There is also a semi-automatic mode known as shutter-priority, often seen as an 'S' or 'Tv' on the settings dial. This is useful, especially if the shutter speed is vital to the type of photography you're doing, such as action. You simply select the shutter speed you want, and the camera will choose the most suitable aperture and/or ISO combination to give you a good exposure. So, you have some control (specifically over the shutter speed), but you're letting the camera do some of the thinking for you. This is great if you need to work swiftly.

How do I know which shutter speed to use?
It depends on a mixture of your creative ambition and technical challenges. Subjects such as wildlife and action require fast shutter speeds, typically 1/250sec or faster (up to 1/8000sec). In low-light conditions or when being creative with blur, you'll need slower shutter speeds. You have to consider how slow you can handhold your camera without introducing unwanted camera shake. This could be as slow as 1/125sec, depending on your steadiness, the weight and ergonomics of your camera, whether you're using image stabilization, and so on. The best approach is to experiment and find what your thresholds are.

What's B mode?
B is short for 'bulb' mode, which you'll need for long exposures. Your camera's shutter will remain open for as long as you keep the shutter button pressed. This is useful for exposure times extending beyond a second or two.

So, I just hold the shutter down, right?
Technically yes, but if you do that, you will undoubtedly introduce camera movement. Even the slightest jiggle of the camera while holding it will register as unwanted motion blur. This is why you'll need a remote trigger. This cable connects to your camera, so you don't have to touch it. The shutter will remain open if you keep the remote trigger pressed. Many modern cameras allow you to connect to an app on your phone via Wi-Fi or Bluetooth, which often features a remote trigger function. It's reasonable to say some are better than others.

If you're using a DSLR (a camera with a mirror – see page 16), you'll need to set this into the locked position before making a long exposure, as even the vibration of the mirror moving can register as motion blur. It's a faff, but it's got to be done.

I'll need a tripod too, right?
Absolutely. A tripod is vital, as there's no way you'll be able to hold a camera steady during a long exposure. In some cases, you may get away with resting your camera on something solid, such as a wall, but you'll be reliant on it being in the right place for your composition, which is unlikely.

SHUTTER SPEED COMPARISON

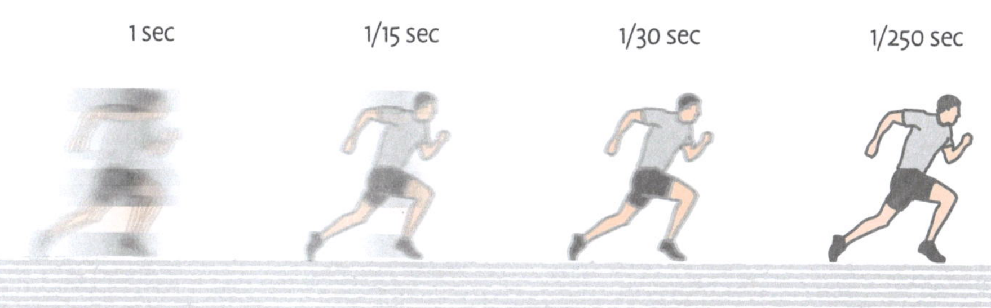

What is flash sync and what does it have to do with shutter speed?

On most consumer cameras (with a focal plane shutter), you may notice there's a fastest shutter speed with which you can use flash, typically 1/125sec to 1/500sec. This is the maximum flash sync speed; you can use speeds that are slower than this, but anything faster will result in a black band across your image. It's one good reason for using a leaf shutter (see page 183), as you can use any shutter speed you want. Sadly, it's not popular and features in only a few cameras.

Why?

Imagine your camera's shutter has two doors. One opens when you start an exposure and moves across the image sensor. To finish the exposure, the second door will start to move across the sensor to close. It'll do all this in a fraction of a second. So, with a fast shutter speed such as 1/250sec, the second door will start closing before the first door has moved all the way across the sensor, meaning there won't be any moment in time when the entire sensor is exposed. For flash photography, you need the whole sensor to be exposed at some point to capture the flash. Typically, that'll be with shutter speeds that are 1/250sec or slower and why you'll see a black band when you use flash with faster shutter speeds.

Has this got anything to do with rear curtain sync?

Yes, it has. Rear or second-curtain sync is a great way to add a creative twist to your work. Unless otherwise instructed, your camera will fire a flash at the beginning of an exposure, which, in most cases, is fine. However, if you're using a slightly slower shutter speed such as 1/15sec, your camera will record the flash and some of the ambient light (depending on how much there is). Now, you can instruct your camera to fire the flash at the end of an exposure rather than the start, hence the name rear (or second) curtain sync.

Wedding photographers frequently use this technique on the dance floor – the flash effectively freezes the action, but the slow-ish exposure also captures the vibe of the event and the warm glow of disco lights. Any motion blur that's also recorded adds to the dynamic energy. Even better, using second-curtain sync creates a trail of motion blur with the subject appearing sharp at the end.

FLASH SYNC

Rear curtain
(second curtain)

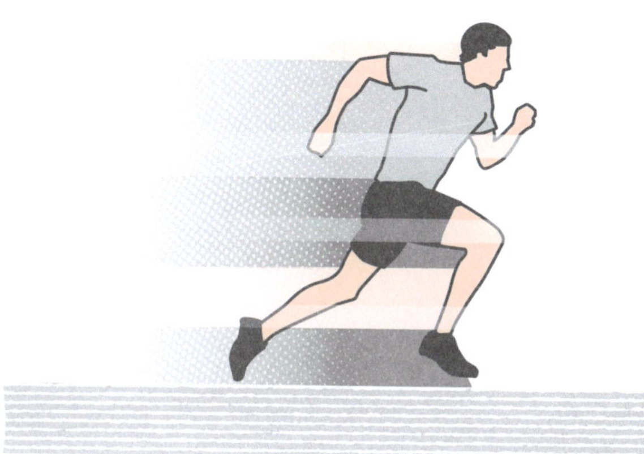

Front curtain
(default)

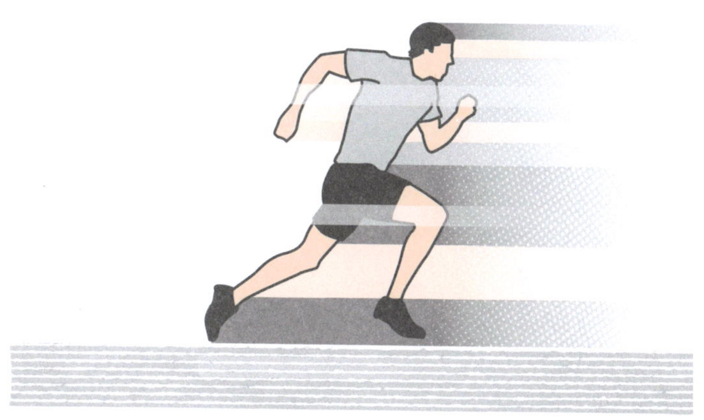

Aperture

Your lens's aperture is basically the hole in the lens that lets light pass through it. It's made up of blades that open and close. These blades can be changed to determine the size of the hole. The size of the hole is measured using f-numbers. A big hole (e.g., f/2.8) lets in more light, while a small hole (e.g., f/22) lets in less light. The hole size affects how much light passes through the lens and, crucially, how the image will look. It impacts the depth of field, which in turn has a massive impact on how much of your image will appear sharp and focused, and so the aperture becomes a vital part of your creative process and thinking.

What is depth of field?
Depth of field is a term that describes the amount of image in front of and beyond the point of critical focus that also appears acceptably sharp. The size of this sharp zone varies depending on the size of your lens's aperture. For example, a small hole will create a deep depth of field where more of the image will appear acceptably sharp, while a large hole will create a shallow depth of field where only a tiny part of an image will appear sharp.

How do I use this in practice?
How you choose to use it depends on what you're shooting. Generally speaking, landscape photographers aspire to produce super-sharp images, so that rocks in the foreground appear as sharp as the distant horizon. They do this by using a very small aperture such as f/22, which gives them a deep depth of field. On the flip side, portrait photographers typically want to avoid distracting backgrounds and create some separation between the subject and the background. They do this by using a super-wide aperture such as f/2.8, which will create a very shallow depth of field where only a sliver of the image appears sharp.

Does the aperture have anything to do with bokeh?
Your lens's aperture is composed of blades that form the iris (hole), which allows light through. The hole size can vary depending on which aperture you select (measured in f-numbers). The number of blades in the lens can vary from model to model; the more there are, the rounder the hole will be, and this will also influence how the bokeh will appear (see page 30).

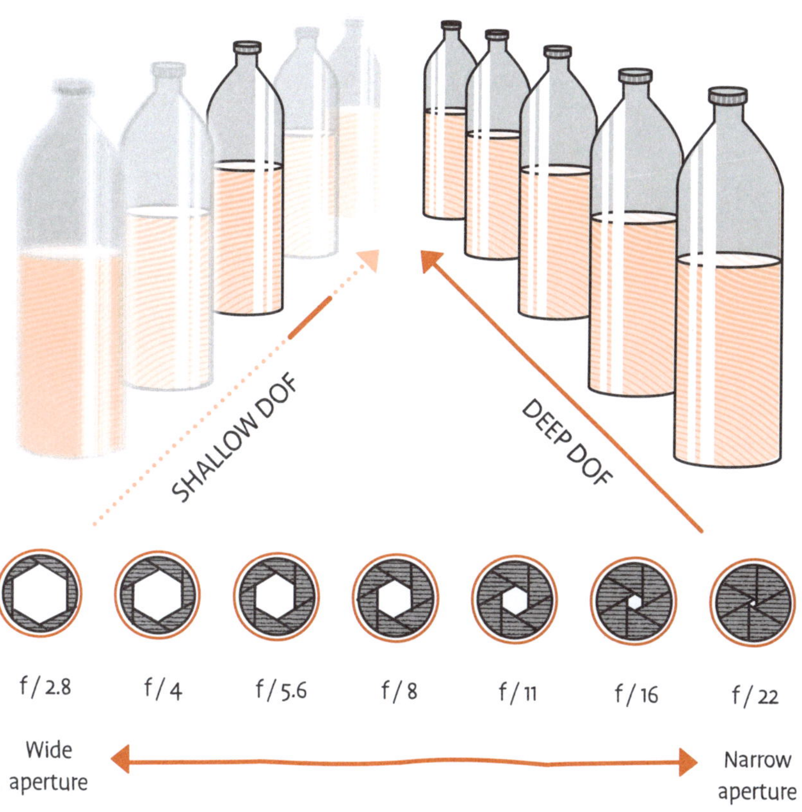
DEPTH OF FIELD
SHALLOW DOF
DEEP DOF
f / 2.8
f / 4
f / 5.6
f / 8
f / 11
f / 16
f / 22
Wide aperture
Narrow aperture

ISO

ISO stands for the International Organization for Standardization, which is an organization that sets international standards for all sorts of measurements. However, in the context of photography, it relates to the third side of the exposure triangle and the sensitivity of your light-sensitive material.

In the days of film, once you'd chosen your film stock and loaded it into your camera, you were stuck with the same ISO for the duration of your 24 or 36 frames. Typically, film came in ISO 100, 200, 400 and 800, and even as high as 3200. Higher-ISO films were more sensitive to light and useful in low-light situations but would also produce very grainy images. Photos made with ISO 3200 film looked like they were made of thousands of dots.

How does this relate to digital cameras?

Increasing the ISO increases your sensor's sensitivity to light and is a great way to get you out of a low-light pickle. However, with digital cameras, you can change the ISO anytime you want, typically with a dial. As with film, there is a change in the image quality: the higher the ISO, the more digital noise will appear in your image. This is similar to film grain (see above), and the higher you crank the ISO, the noisier it becomes.

How high can you go?

You'll be able to go a lot higher than film was ever able to take you. Some cameras have such amazing high-ISO performance that you can take a photo in near darkness. A maximum of ISO 102,400 is commonplace. However, images rarely look good with such high ISOs. Do some tests, find out what is acceptable to you and have that as your cap – you may be surprised how high that is.

How does this relate to the exposure triangle?

Like aperture and shutter speed, ISO is an integral part of an exposure. However, it has less impact on creative decision-making and is unlike the other sides of the triangle. ISO won't affect depth of field and motion blur for instance, but it will reveal noise when it gets a bit high. But don't underestimate its usefulness in reconciling all the compromises you need to consider when making an exposure.

Should I use Auto ISO?

Auto ISO is a little like aperture and shutter-priority modes in that you effectively let the camera decide the right ISO for you. You can cap how high it will go based on your experiments (see above). It can be useful, but it can also be irritating if you're trying to take complete control of your exposure.

What is noise reduction?

A way of reducing noise in image-editing software such as Adobe Lightroom and Affinity Photo. It works well if used cautiously.

UNDERSTANDING NOISE

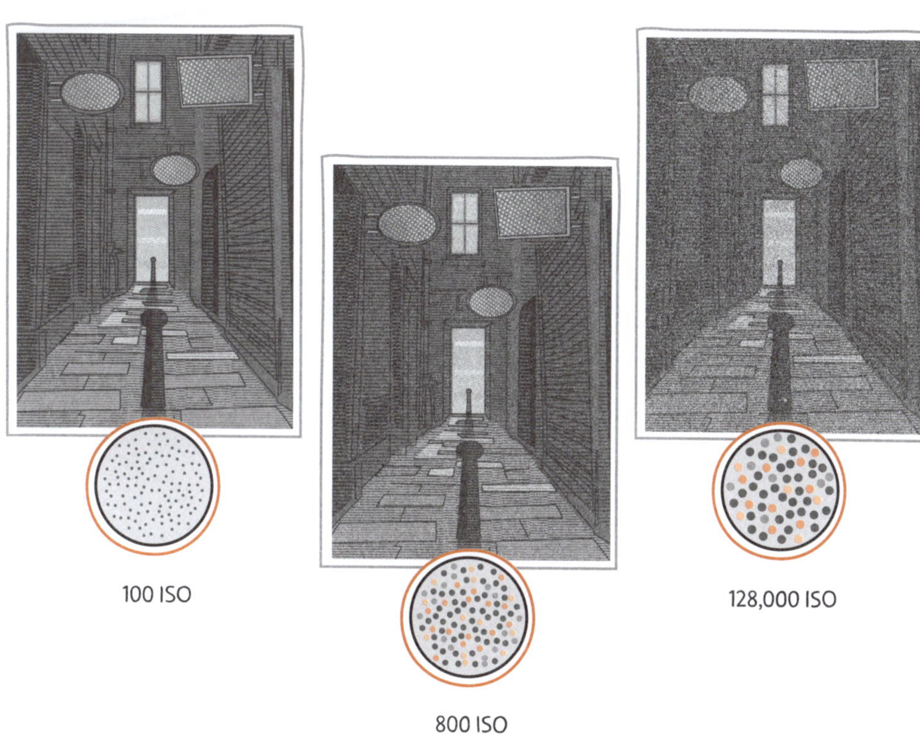

Advanced exposure

What's bracketing?
It's the act of taking several photographs, typically three in rapid succession, at three different exposures. The idea is that you can choose the best one retrospectively. It's not a bad idea, however, it doesn't work for all subjects: portraiture, wildlife, street or action photography rely on split-second timing to capture a moment in time or the subtle nuance of an expression. Taking three shots at different exposures simply won't work. Most cameras have a setting that will automatically 'bracket' for you. This can be as annoying as it is helpful, especially if you forget to turn it off, and you're left trying to figure out why your exposures are all over the place.

What does 'exposing to the right' mean?
It's a technique in which you deliberately overexpose an image to make it appear brighter while also being careful not to lose any detail in the highlights. Imagine the histogram is clumped to the right but not clipped off the graph's edge. The technique exploits the fact that digital sensors perform better at the lighter end of the tonal scale. The exposure can be corrected afterwards in image-editing software and reduces the potential for noise in shadow areas.

What about raw and JPEG files?
A raw file is an unprocessed, uncompressed image file made using data directly from your camera's sensor. While it might be a good format for the best quality, it will not typically look as good straight out of the camera as a JPEG. You'll have to edit in a raw processor such as Adobe Lightroom. On the other hand, a JPEG will have been processed and compressed by your camera. Superficially, it may appear better straight out of the camera, but the in-camera processing and compression leave you less to work with. In many cases, this is fine. Editing in raw is also a non-destructive process, so you don't risk destroying the original image, which you can easily do when editing a JPEG.

BRACKETING

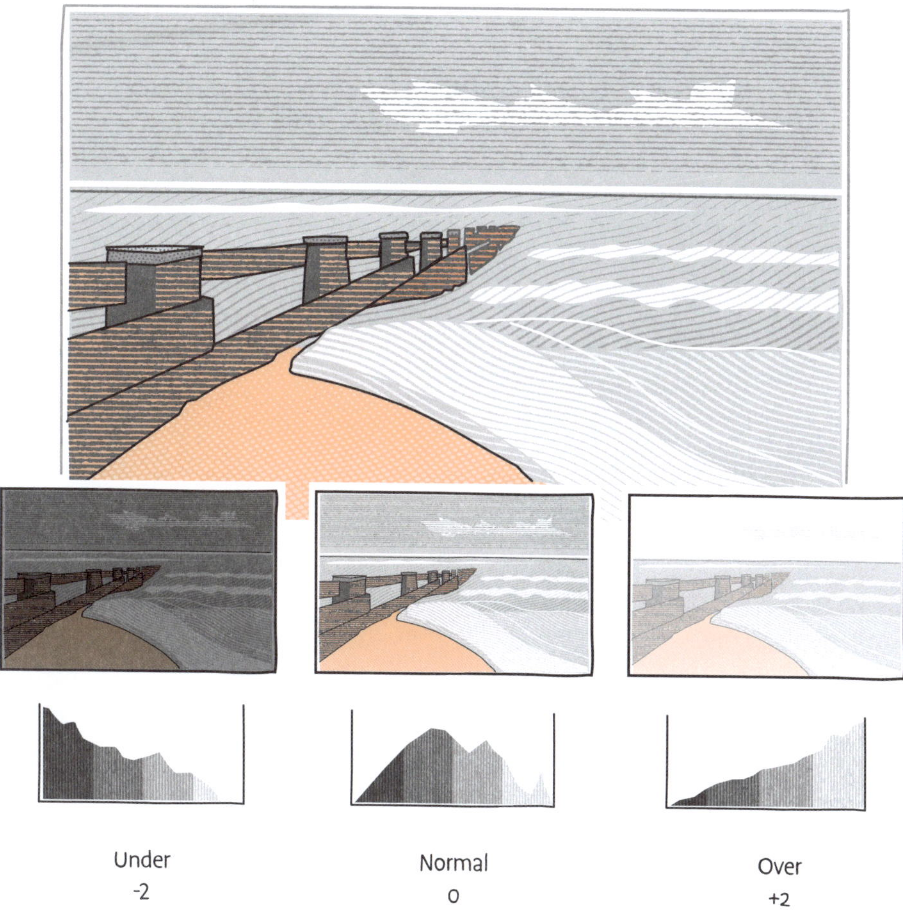

Light

Light is the essence, the essential ingredient, of a photograph, so much so that the word 'photography' literally means 'painting with light' – it's derived from the Greek words 'phos' (light) and 'graphê' (drawing). Learning to notice, appreciate and understand how to use light in your creative photography is vital.

How do I get started?

Perhaps the best place to get started in your journey of light appreciation is to simply start looking and take the time to notice in a mindful, contemplative way how light falls throughout the day; notice how it changes colour and intensity, how the weather affects it, how it changes from season to season and in different parts of the world. Then look at artificial light and notice how, for example, the strip lights in a corporate office look compared with the warm glow of a bedside lamp.

What kind of light is there?

Let's start with a hard light such as the midday sun on a bright day, which can be brutal with characteristics such as strong shadows and high contrast. While many photographers avoid this kind of light, it can be wonderfully expressive when used creatively.

On the flip side, you'll notice more diffused light. The even tones of a diffused or 'soft' light have the opposite effect to the savage rays of hard light. Natural light is usually softer due to clouds, which act as a massive diffuser.

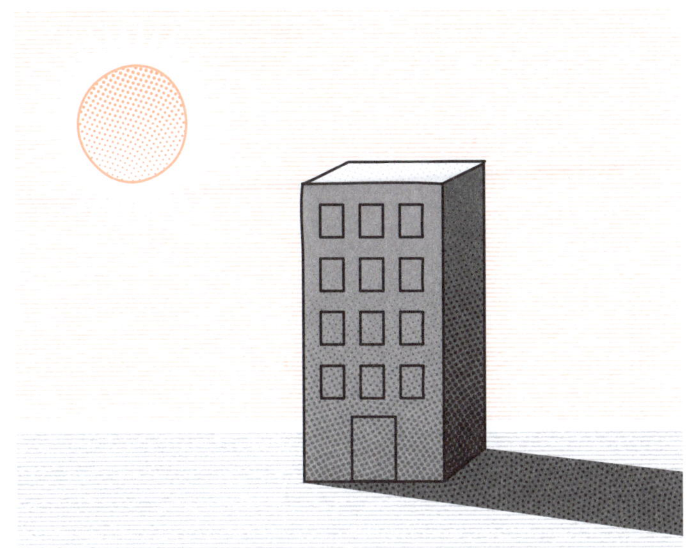

Hard light

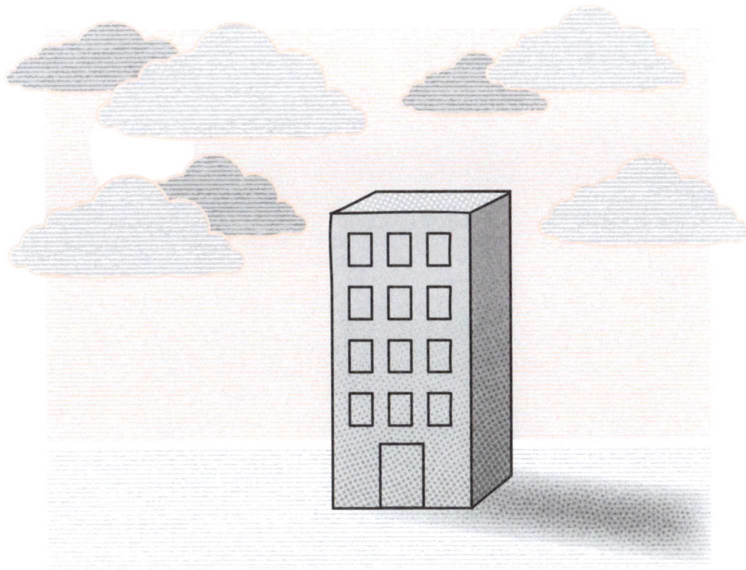

Soft light

What's colour balance got to do with light?
It's not just the quality of light that changes through the day. Light's colour varies from hour to hour too. You may have heard photographers talking about the 'blue hour', the 'golden hour' and so on; they're talking about the quality and the colour of light. They will sometimes get up at ungodly hours to take advantage of it.

The Kelvin scale is used to measure the 'colour' of light.

Is this what white balance is for?
Yes, you must be aware of white balance and adjust it in your settings. However, in most cases, simply setting it to auto will be fine. If you're shooting raw files, which you probably should be doing, you can tweak the white balance at the editing stage, but as with everything, it's best to try and get it right in camera.

Scroll through your white balance settings, taking pictures as you go, and notice how the colour of the photographs change.

Some professional photographers, especially those working in advertising, fashion and so on, will often use a colour-checker card. They'll take a reference shot that includes the cards, and this 'reference' shot can be used at the editing stage to ensure the colours are accurate in all the images.

I hear conflicting information about shooting towards the sun...
Shooting into the light, or 'contre-jour' if you want to sound cool, can be a super-creative way to make your images shine. However, it's not without its challenges. First, your camera will become totally confused and try to compensate for all that light spilling into the frame, so it'll most likely underexpose your image. So, switch to manual mode or use exposure compensation to effectively overexpose by a stop or three.

Why do it?
Once you've sorted out the exposure, shooting into the sun can produce a lovely backlight, adding depth and radiance to a shot, along with wonderful rim-light effects. It works well for portraits.

Do I need my lens hood for this?
Lens hoods are designed to help eliminate lens flare, which is one of the effects of shooting towards the light. The hood shields the front of the lens from being hit directly by the sun, which does the job of getting rid of the flare.

TIME OF DAY

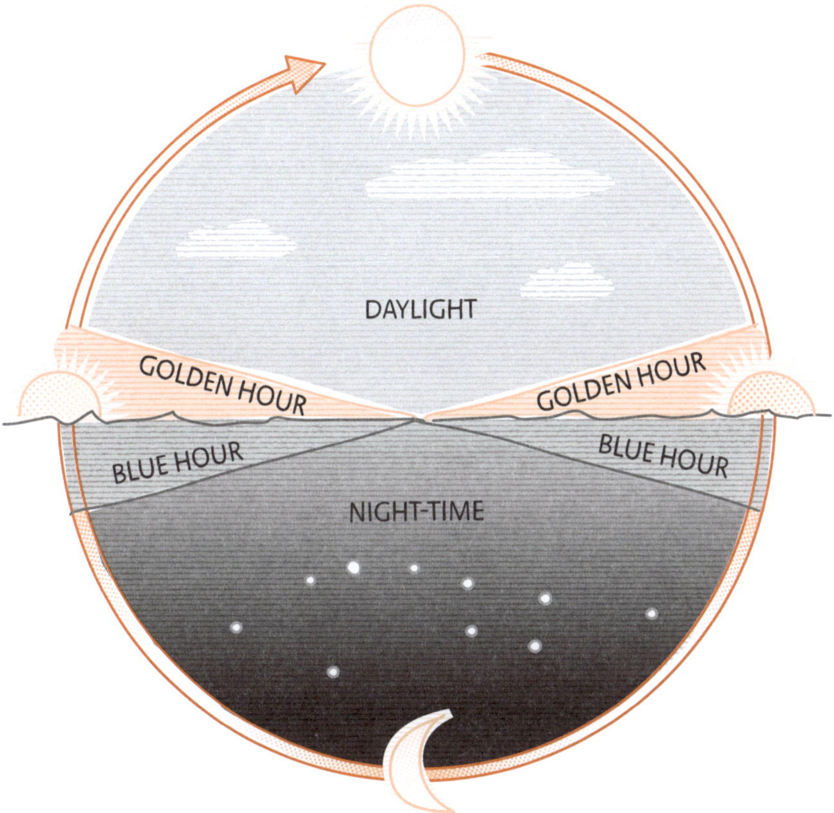

DAYLIGHT

GOLDEN HOUR

GOLDEN HOUR

BLUE HOUR

BLUE HOUR

NIGHT-TIME

KELVIN SCALE

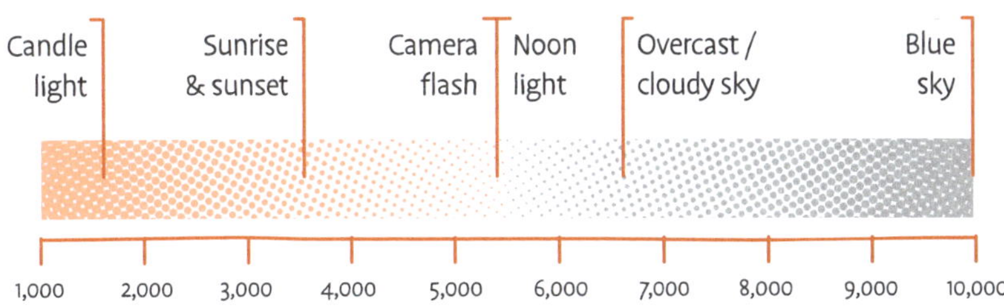

So, we've talked about the various types of natural light and ways to think about and appreciate its qualities and incorporate that into your workflow, but there are many ways to add and control light using artificial sources, such as flashguns, studio lights, continuous LED lights, and so on.

What are they?
Let's take a look at some common artifical light sources:

On-camera flash
On-camera flash is a flashlight built into the camera and activated by a pop-up device, or an external device attached via the camera's hotshoe, found on the top of the camera. They vary wildly in quality and cost. Typically, they tend to produce a harder, less-flattering light, in part because the direction of the light source is from the camera rather than to the side, making it difficult to 'sculpt' light. However, they can be tethered from the camera and fired remotely using a wireless connection between the camera and the flashgun.

Studio lights
Artificial studio lights are found in just about every photo studio. They provide consistent and adjustable lighting in a very controlled environment. They come in all shapes and sizes and have a wide range of prices. Unlike on-camera flash, studio lights can be positioned on stands away from the camera, and photographers often use multiple lights which they position in such a way as to sculpt the light to their creative fancy.

Until relatively recently, studio lights were nearly always flashlights or strobes, but these days LED lights are becoming more popular as technology in that area advances. The advantage of LEDs is that you can see the effect of the light immediately, but they can struggle if lots of light is needed.

Regardless of which lights a studio photographer uses, the art of lighting is a highly refined skill. Perhaps the best place to start is by booking a session at a rental studio or, better still, a lighting workshop. If the bug bites you, there are plenty of great starter kits.

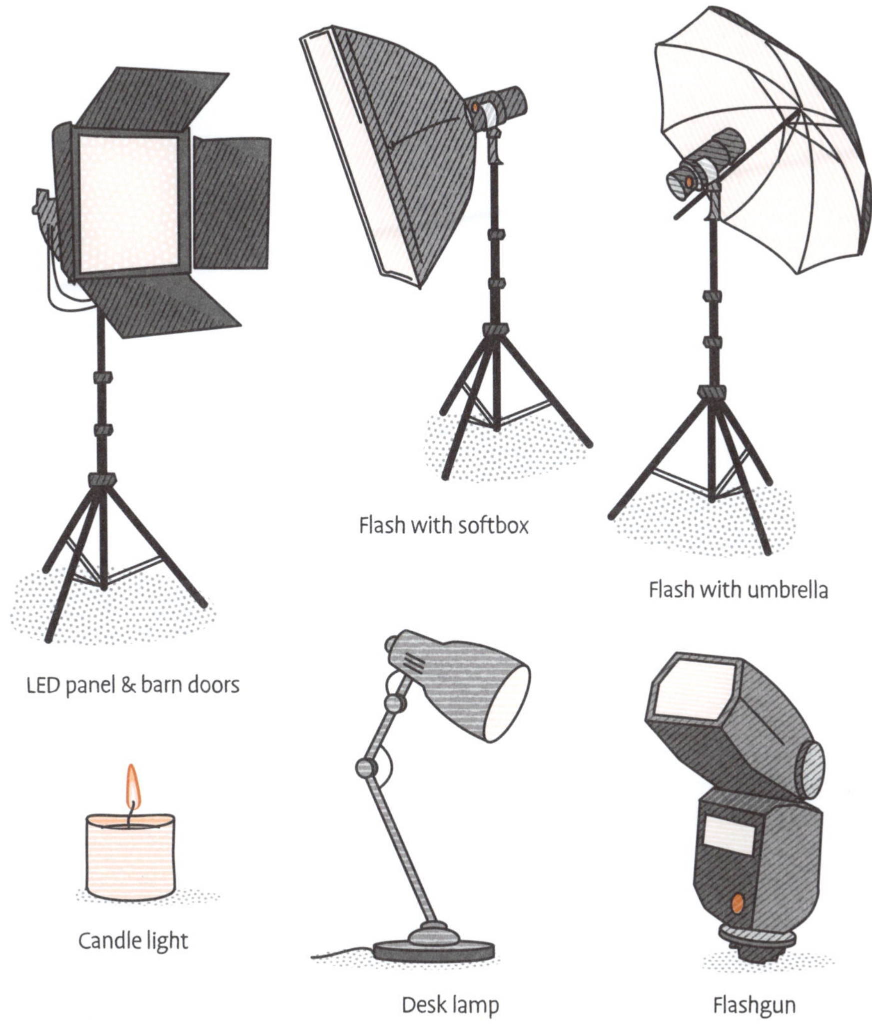

Modifiers

In nearly every studio, you'll also see a bunch of umbrellas, softboxes, octoboxes, reflectors, and so on. These are all modifiers, and their different shapes, sizes and surfaces will reflect, diffuse, block and change the characteristics of the light. So, as well as determining the best position of the lights, a decent studio photographer will also be able to control the characteristics, making it harder or softer, feathered or whatever is needed to reflect the creative vision. This is also highly skilled work.

Composition

Why is composition important?
What you choose to include and exclude in the viewfinder or screen of your camera is one of the fundamental aspects of making an image. You're effectively commenting on the world and telling stories by deciding what to photograph. But it's not just what you include or not – it's also how you arrange the elements in the frame.

How do I control that?
By crouching down, or standing up tall, or moving to the side a little. Sometimes, the smallest movement can make a big difference to the relationship of objects in a scene. You could even try using a different focal length, exploring new angles and so on. The most important thing to do is to look at what's in the frame. Don't just focus on the main subject, but look at the relationship of the elements, even stuff that's seemingly insignificant in the background. Carefully scan the edges of your frame before clicking the shutter.

But I've never studied 'composition' at art school – how do I get started?
Simply start looking. Some people can find a harmonious composition easily, while others have to work a little harder. The great American photographer Edward Weston famously said, 'Consulting the rules of composition before taking a photo is like consulting the rules of gravity before going for a walk'. However, he was a genius, and it clearly came naturally to him. So, if you're struggling to get started, we'll look at some of the 'rules' and guides over the next couple of pages.

Aren't all the rules super-complicated?
They can be. The 'established' rules of composition generally hark back to the theories rooted in the 'golden mean', which is connected to the number phi. You can see examples of this in painting and architecture, even the structure of musical scores. You can also witness it in nature, from nautilus shells and curling ferns to spiralling far-flung galaxies in outer space. However, as fascinating as the maths can be, basic guides such as the rule of thirds approximate the golden mean and are a lot easier to use.

How do I put this into practice?
Over the next couple of pages, we'll look at some things to consider when you're contemplating composition, and we'll explore some of the 'rules' and guides that might help you get started.

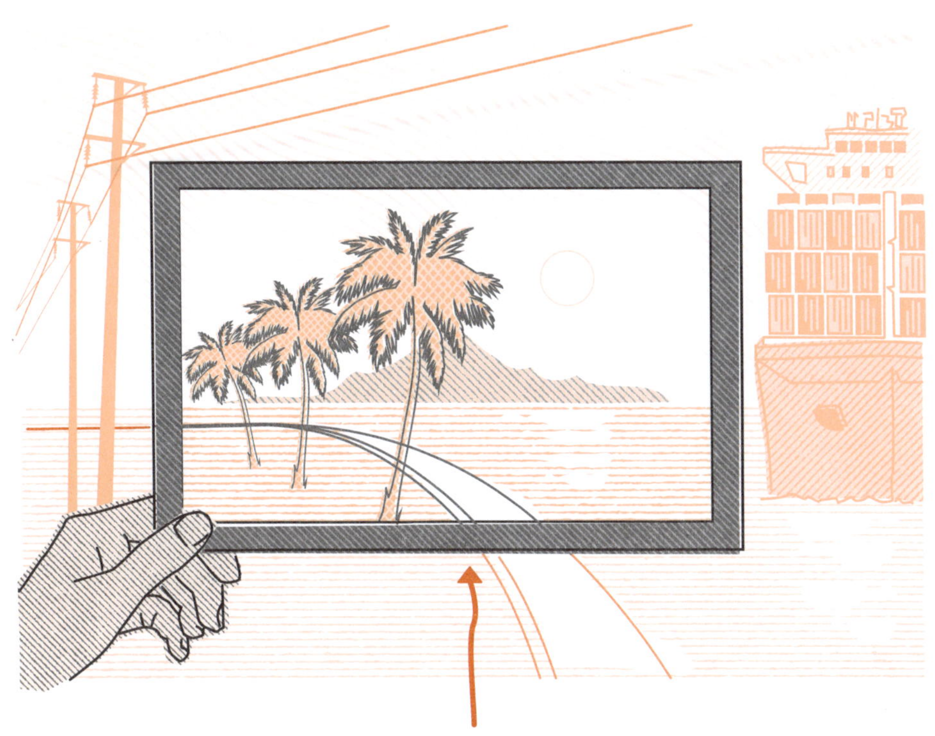

Compose your shot carefully and you can remove unwanted elements from the frame

Is the rule of thirds a good place to start?

It is a good place to start but think of it as a guide rather than a rule. Rules can become stifling, and plenty of great photographs don't use the 'rules'.

Okay, but how does the 'guide' of thirds work?

Imagine your frame is divided into nine rectangles made up of two vertical lines and two horizontal lines. The idea is to then place important parts of a scene at the point where these lines intersect. The eye is naturally drawn to that part of the image; it approximates the golden mean. It can also be a good idea to position a horizontal line either a third up from the bottom of the frame or a third down from the top. Generally, it'll feel more balanced, although it can also be a little boring if used too rigorously.

So, you just have to imagine the lines, right?

That's the idea. However, you can activate a grid overlay on your camera's screen, which can be very useful when you start. Even most smartphone cameras have this setting. In time though, you'll find it just comes naturally.

What about leading lines?

They're another 'classic' aspect of composition to consider. They pretty much do what they say on the tin: look for elements in a scene that can be used to draw the viewer's gaze into the frame. This will make the photo more engaging. Look for things such as railings, roads and paths, cables, the gesture of an arm or anything else that leads the viewer's eye.

And the 'frame within the frame' rule?

It's not a rule as such, but just like leading lines, it's a question of looking for elements in a scene that can be used as a framing device. A window is an obvious example. Using the window gives the viewer some context and something to look through, which also helps make the image more engaging.

RULES OF COMPOSITION

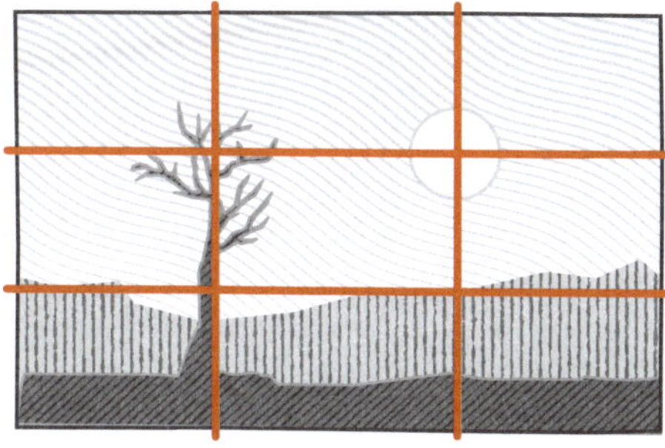

Rule of thirds

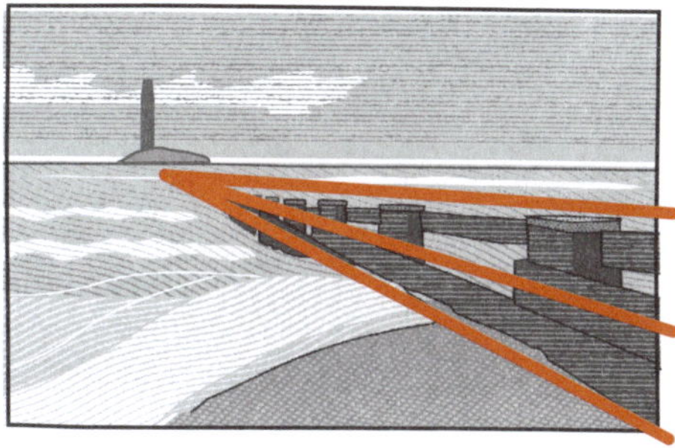

Leading lines

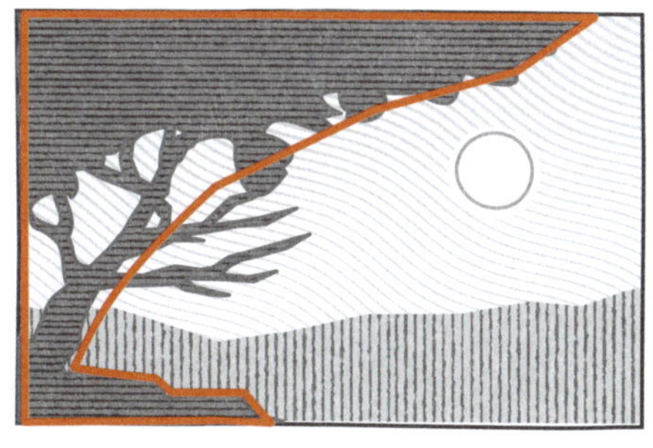

Frame within a frame

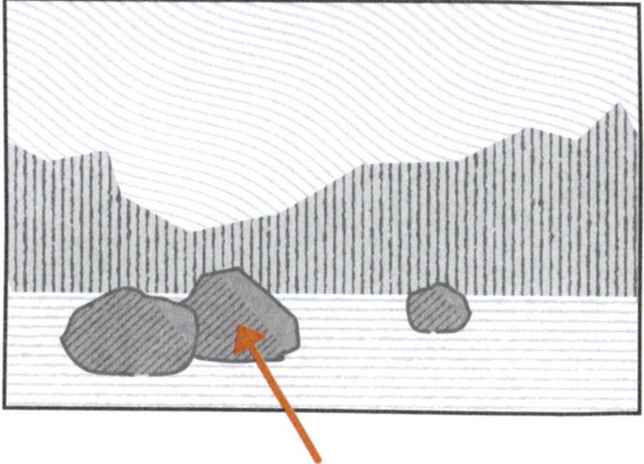

Foreground interest

What's negative space?
It's an invaluable aspect of composition that you should be aware of. Negative space is all about the parts of an image that aren't the subject and that don't have anything in them. This could be the sky or the area of nothing between two objects. This space also makes a shape, and it's important to 'see' and notice this space, as it's also part of the picture.

And active space?
Building on the idea of negative space, think about how you can incorporate this into your action shots. Despite a photo being a still, static moment captured in a split second, it is still possible to convey a sense of energy and motion. One way to do this – and to help make your images tell a story – is to give a moving object or person space, typically negative space, to move into. So, imagine a runner moving from left to right across the frame – it makes more 'visual sense' for them to have space to run into on the right side, so when positioning yourself for the shot, do so in a way that allows you to place the runner to the left of the frame.

The same principle can be used when photographing portraits, especially when the subject is not looking directly at the camera. Follow the direction of your subject's gaze and leave space in the frame for them to 'look' into.

Is colour important to composition?
Absolutely. Colour can be a great way to add resonance to an image. Complementary colours such as yellow and blue or red and cyan can be particularly effective. Keep a keen eye open for exciting colour palettes when you're out and about.

What about the rule of odds?
If you have control over the objects in your image, such as when shooting a still life, try and work with an odd number of objects. Generally speaking, it's much easier to make a more harmonious arrangement. Take four apples and attempt to arrange them pleasingly in the frame, then take one away and notice how it feels easier to make a balanced composition. There are plenty of examples when the opposite is true, so it's something to ponder and be aware of rather than to live and die by.

ACTIVE SPACE

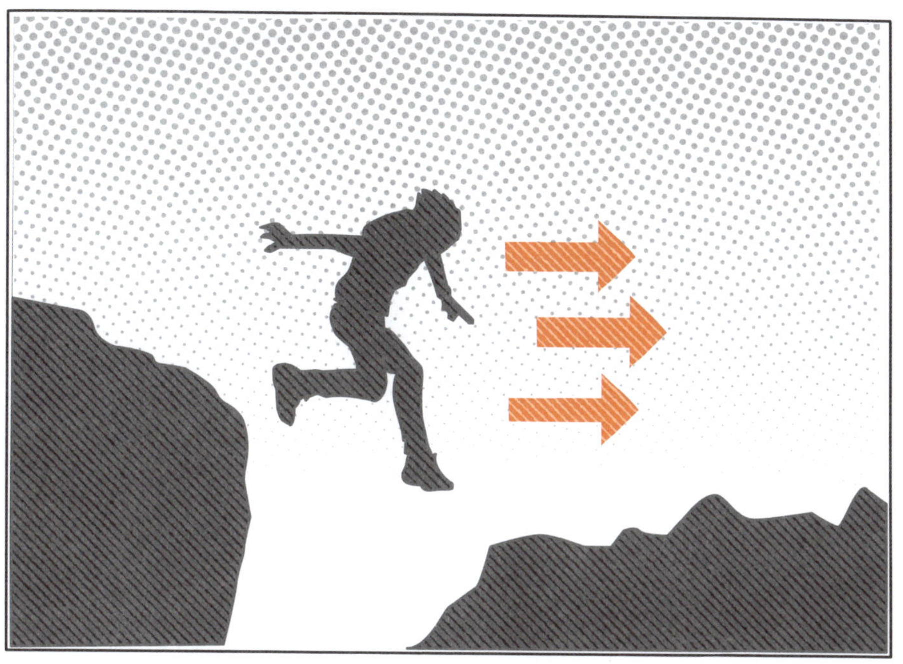

What about aspect ratio?

We generally think of the frame of a photograph in terms of a rectangle, although there's no reason why we have to think that way – squares and even circles can work just as well. That said, it's worth mentioning aspect ratio, and it's something to think about. In the first instance, there's the native aspect ratio of your camera to consider – the proportions of your sensor determine this. Full-frame sensors are based on the 3:2 aspect ratio, the same proportions as a 35mm film frame – this has evolved into the photography 'standard'. However, there are a bunch of other aspects ratios to contemplate too. Here's a round up:

5:4

This used to be the standard photographic format, based on a sheet of 5x4 film used in large-format cameras. This aspect ratio is also reflected in the 8x10 print, which is still a perennial favourite with off-the-shelf photo frames.

1:1

The mighty square! This is an interesting format. Some argue that working with a square frame is more challenging than a rectangle – try it and see. Of course, social media platforms such as Instagram have popularized the ratio.

16:9

The standard widescreen proportions. This is great for capturing wide vistas and giving them a panoramic vibe. Naturally, widescreen TVs have made this a familiar and mainstream format. If you crop an image to this format, you'll be wasting some precious pixels, so you could try stitching images to make a panorama in this ratio – see page 100 to see how. Be bold and try a vertical orientation in this format. This too has been popularized by social media platforms, especially TikTok videos and Instagram Reels.

Which way should I hold my camera?

It's totally up to you and your creative vision. Convention dictates that it's horizontal for landscapes and vertical for portraits, to the extent that people even use the terms 'landscape' and 'portrait' to describe orientation. That's bonkers! There are plenty of great vertically oriented landscapes and horizontally oriented portraits.

Break the rules!

While the guides, rules and advice in the previous pages are helpful, especially if you're new to image-making, they are not to live and die by. There are plenty of amazing examples of amazing rule-breaking pictures throughout the history of photography. Disregard them with abandon.

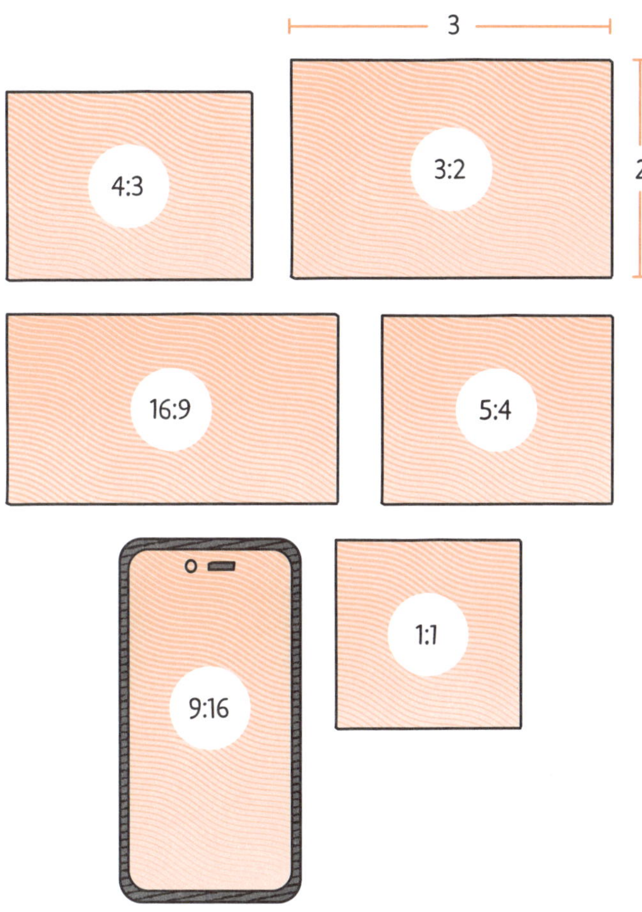
ASPECT RATIO
3
2
4:3
3:2
16:9
5:4
9:16
1:1

Focusing

What's the best way to focus?

It depends on your subject, but start with the basics. Typically, you'll have the option to use autofocus (AF) or manual focus (MF). In most cases, autofocus is good, but there may be one or two situations when switching to manual focus is better.

In autofocus mode, you simply half-press the shutter release, and your camera will start to focus on the specified point. This point can be moved using your thumb on a mini navigation button; the number of positions you can move it to depends on your camera. Alternatively, you focus on the area you want to be sharp and then, keeping the shutter release half-pressed, you recompose your shot. It's fiddly at first, but you get the hang of it.

Some photographers prefer using a back button rather than half-pressing the shutter release; double-check if your camera can do this and try it out. Some love it, while others hate it.

What about continuous mode?

Switching your focus mode to 'continuous focusing' means that while the shutter is half-pressed, the camera will continue focusing, even if you move it. It's helpful when you want to track your subjects, such as when shooting sports, action and wildlife photography.

And face detection?

Another cool feature found on some cameras. This technology is getting pretty good, and it's a more useful feature than it used to be. The camera uses advanced technology to identify faces in a scene. It'll latch onto it and track it, ensuring it's always sharp. Well, that's the theory.

What about a touchscreen?

Touchscreen is an increasingly common feature on digital cameras nowadays – check your manual to make sure it's available on yours. Essentially, you activate the camera's LCD screen, and it will focus wherever you touch it. In some situations, it's useful, and in others it's annoying.

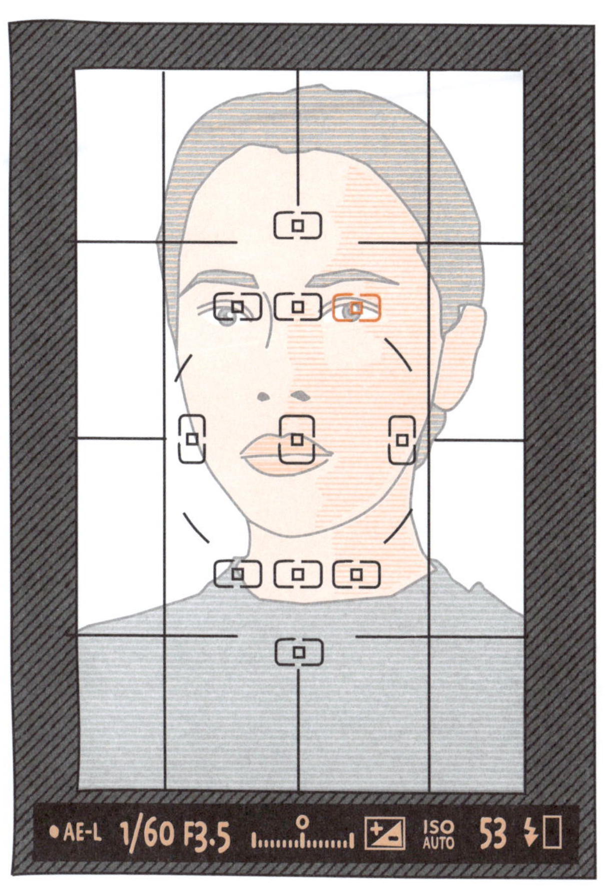

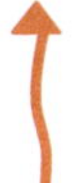

For portraits, manually select the focus point that sits over the nearest eye

How do I focus manually and why should I bother?

Back in the day, all cameras were manual focus and focusing was achieved by twisting a ring on the lens barrel until the image appeared sharp. Some optical features helped assist this, such as split prisms and micro prisms, but these are basic compared to today's standard. Manual focusing is still useful today despite all the fancy technological advances with autofocus. Some situations are still a challenge for autofocus, especially in low-light situations.

Manually focusing on a digital camera is typically just a case of switching to MF and moving the focus ring on the lens. Some nifty focus aids will help you, though. You can often zoom in to see a magnified view of the area you want to focus on. You can also activate a focus peak highlight preview, highlighting all areas of the image that will appear sharp.

What's the diopter for?

This is the little dial found near the viewfinder on your camera. Use it to correct the viewfinder to your optical vision. This is very useful if you wear glasses.

Does it have to be in focus?

Regardless of the method or technology you choose for focusing, paying careful attention to what's sharp or not is a vital part of the creative process. You should practise and hone your focusing skills, so they become instinctive. The great French photographer Henri Cartier-Bresson famously stated, 'Sharpness is a bourgeois concept'. Instead, he emphasized the importance of capturing the decisive moment over things like critical focusing. He may have a point, but these days with so much technology to hand, you can most likely strive for both. There is much to love about Cartier-Bresson's quote, attitude and images, but don't use this as an excuse for sloppy focusing.

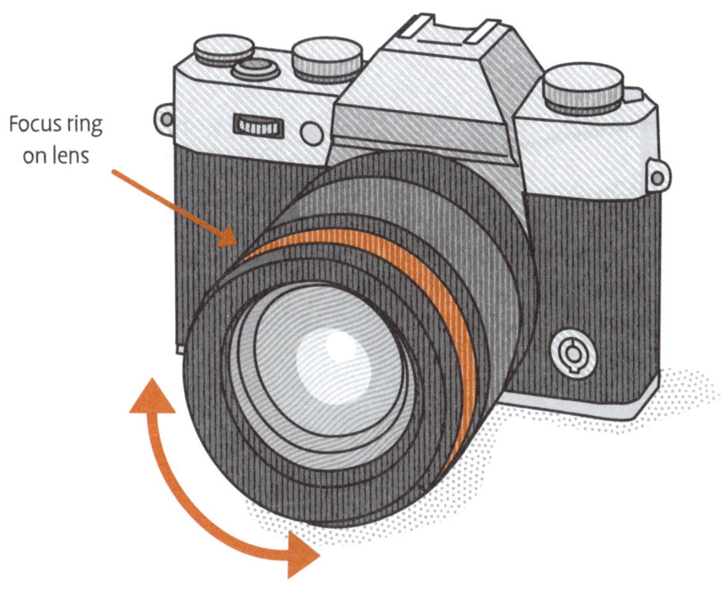
Focus ring
on lens

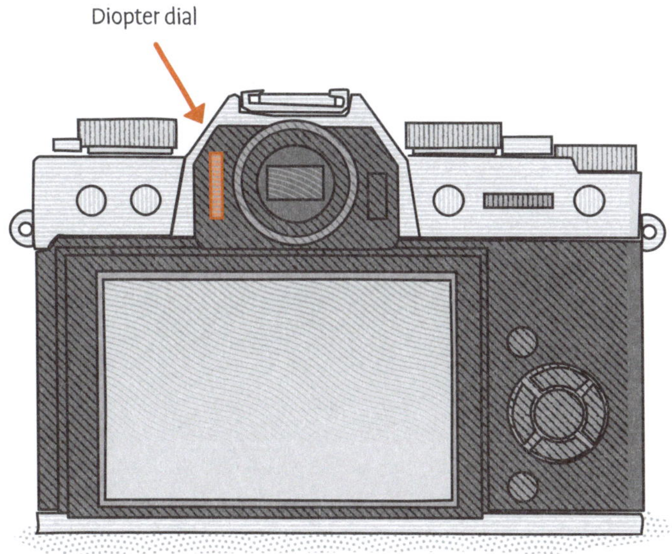
Diopter dial

What the heck is hyperfocal focusing?
It is complicated but also useful for some types of photography. Hyperfocal focusing is a technique used to maximize the depth of field (see page 50), ensuring that as wide a range of distances as possible in a scene appear sharp. The hyperfocal distance is the point of focus that allows for the greatest depth of field possible for a given aperture setting and focal length.

Why use it?
Imagine a landscape where you want a rock in the foreground to appear as sharp as the distant horizon, and ask yourself what you'd focus on. Using the principles of depth of field, you can accurately assume that using a small aperture such as f/16 will give you a deep depth of field and that much of the scene will appear sharp. But where do you focus? This is where using hyperfocal distance focusing can be useful.

How do I do that?
You'll need to consider factors such as your sensor size, focal length and aperture and make some calculations. Urgh, I hear you say, that sounds like way too much to think about, on top of being creative. Well, the good news is that help is on hand. While there are some hyperfocal distance calculation charts which you could print out and keep in your camera bag, there are now a bunch of neat apps that'll do all the work for you. PhotoPills is brilliant. Using an app, you can quickly ascertain that with a specific lens on a specific camera and at a specific aperture, there will be an optimum distance to focus at for maximum (acceptable) sharpness in your scene.

So, with my Fujifilm GFX and 45mm lens, and using an aperture of f/11, I can quickly ascertain that my hyperfocal focus point is 4.73m (15.5ft). Focus on that point, and I'll exploit the depth of field and maximize the apparent sharpness. Hopefully, this includes the rock, but if not, changing my aperture to f/22 might do the job while bringing the hyperfocal point to 2.39m (7.8ft). That should do it.

How do I focus so precisely on a specified distance rather than on an object?
First, switch to manual mode and focus manually. If your lens has a focus scale, use this to set the distance. Sometimes, this can be seen on a scale in the camera's viewfinder or LCD screen. Otherwise, use a tape measure or estimate.

Anything else I should know?
Yes, while most landscape photographers understand the principles of hyperfocal focusing, in reality, they often apply it in more general, intuitive ways. For example, focusing about a third of the way into a scene is usually fairly close. Previewing and checking the sharpness on location means you can see what's happening anyway.

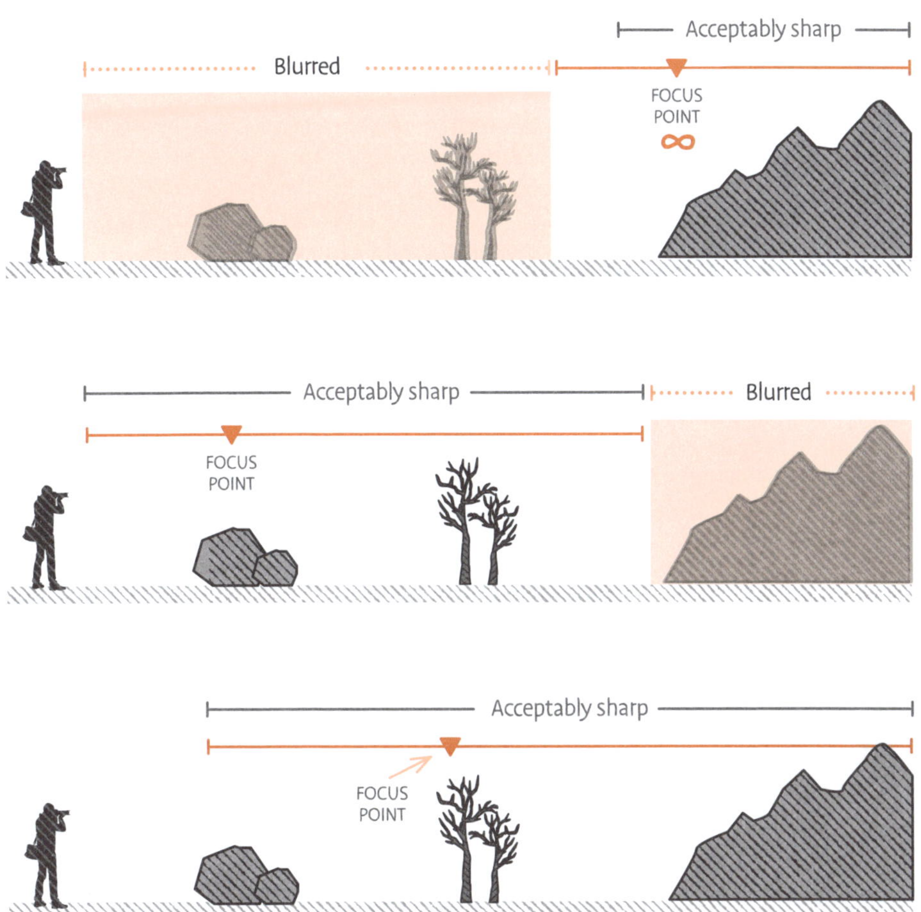

Is it just for landscape photography?
It's mainly used by landscape photographers, but you can use the principles in other types of photography too. Street photographers, in particular, use the technique to quickly capture a split-second moment without faffing around with focusing. They're effectively pre-focusing at the hyperfocal point and working on the assumption that everything beyond that point will be acceptably sharp. It works surprisingly well, although a spot of electrical tape on your focus ring helps prevent accidentally shifting your focus point.

Taking a photo

What's the best way to physically take a photo?

That is a good question and one that's easy to overlook. In the first instance, it's good practice to be thoroughly familiar with your camera's knobs, buttons, dials and menu systems. We cover some of these in other parts of the book, however, knowing how to change settings quickly is vital. Take time to explore your camera's features. Most will allow you to customize buttons and dials for quick access to the features or menu settings you anticipate needing speedy access to. This can be incredibly useful and tailored to your style of photography. For example, sports and wildlife photographers will most likely have their cameras configured differently from landscape or still life photographers.

When you come to press the shutter, the action should feel like a gentle squeeze rather than a harsh stab, the aim being to avoid unwanted camera movement. Even at fast shutter speeds, a heavy-handed jab at the shutter release will cause vibrations that could ruin your shot.

How fast or slow you can handhold a camera largely depends on your steadiness, the weight and ergonomics of your camera and the degree of lens and camera stabilization. Regardless of the speed, try to work out what your slowest speed is and use this as a guide to inform you when to use a tripod, increase the ISO or use artificial light.

How should I hold my camera?

The way you hold and handle your camera is important. The key is stability and ensuring everything is as steady and controlled as possible. This is why the viewfinder can often be a better option than the LCD screen – holding a camera to your eye is way more stable that looking at a screen at arm's length. Look for something to lean on or against, keep your elbows tucked in and let the weight of your equipment flow into your body.

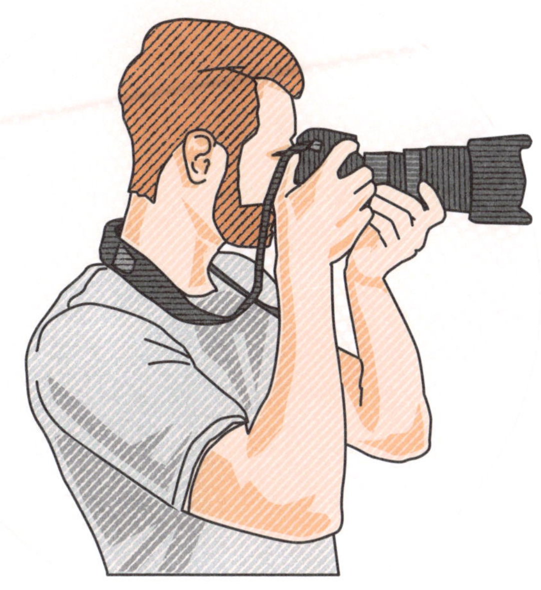

Keep your elbows tucked in and let the weight of your equipment flow into your body

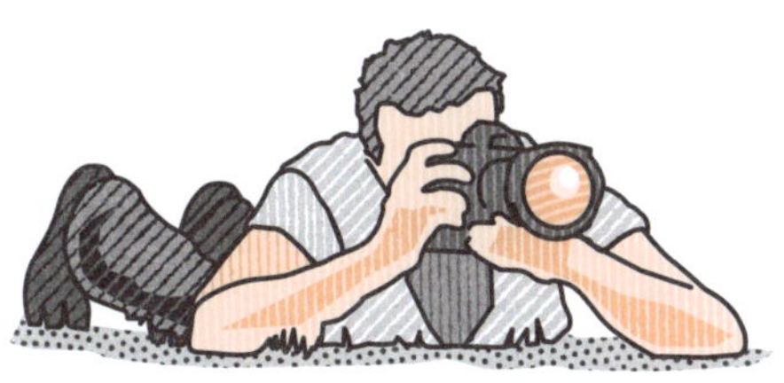

You can kneel or lie down for added stability

Essential skills:
Recap

This chapter is essentially the nuts and bolts of photography – some of the subjects discussed might not be the most fun or creative. However, take the time to make sure you understand the basic principles, and everything else in this book and on your photographic journey will be more enjoyable.

Five top tips

1 Ignore all the fancy modes and specialist settings that most cameras come armed with, and focus on getting to grips with the principles of the exposure triangle.

2 Trust your intuition, especially with certain aspects of photography, such as composition. There are plenty of fine examples of photographs that break all the 'rules' that are sublime nonetheless. The 'rules' are guides to help you on your way, not laws to live and die by.

3 Even when you're not photographing, develop the habit of noticing light. Look for its colour, its strength, its direction, the shadows, and so on.

4 Look at the work of great photographers: there is a lot to learn from studying the history of photography. There are plenty of fine books on the subject.

5 Think of photography as a language. The subjects covered in this chapter are giving you the core skills to express yourself with a camera.

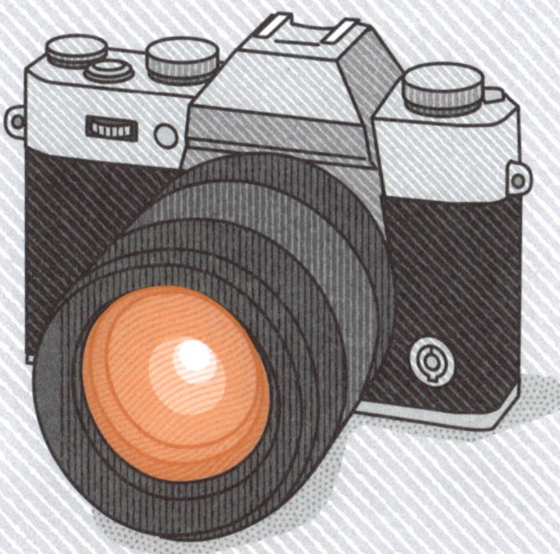

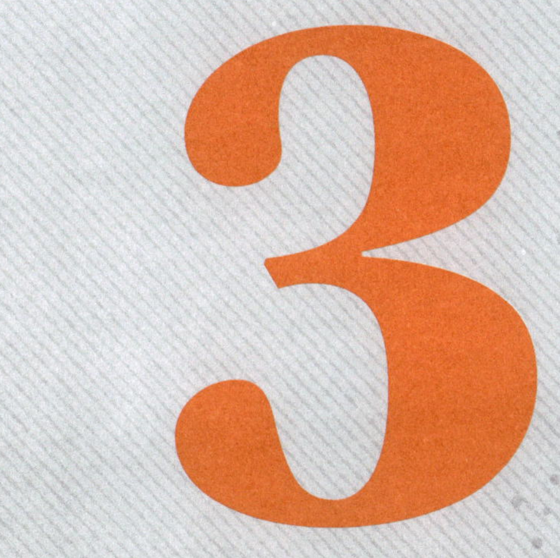

3 CREATIVE TECHNIQUES

HDR explained

What is HDR photography?
HDR stands for high dynamic range. HDR photography is a technique that basically allows you to expand the range of tones in a photograph. Typically, getting a correct exposure is a series of compromises (see exposure triangle on page 40) and you need to decide whether you want detail in the shadow areas or the highlights of your scene, especially if it's a bright day. Generally, you can't have both.

How do I make an HDR image?
Once you've established that you can't get detail in the highlights and shadows in one shot, it's time to think about HDR techniques as an option. The basic premise is to take multiple images at different exposures, some for the highlights and some for the shadows, and then combine them in image-editing software afterwards.

How do I do that?
You'll need to ensure that all the images – typically three to five – are aligned, as the individual images will need to be layered and merged in exact registration with one another later. So, in the first instance, you'll need a tripod. If you use the exposure-bracketing feature that's on most cameras and a remote trigger, you'll be taking the series of images without touching and moving the camera between shots. This will make life easier later. Shoot raw, and then in the digital darkroom, use software to combine the light and dark images into one image with a full range of tones, including detail in the shadows and in the highlights. Dedicated HDR software is available, however mainstream image editors such as Adobe Photoshop offer the functionality too.

When should I use it?
It's up to you! Some photographers never use it, and that's fine, while other photographers overuse it, and that's fine too, although less so. There is a tendency to latch onto seemingly cool techniques like this. The thing is, some people get overzealous, and the results can look awful, especially if the technique shines through and overrides everything else. Like all fancy techniques, if it's obvious it's been used, you've failed. So, restraint is crucial.

If all the shots need to be composed the same, I can't take an HDR action shot...
Correct! It's tricky to make an HDR image of a subject that's moving, as you have to be able to merge several identically composed images. So, subjects such as portraits, wildlife and action are not easy options.

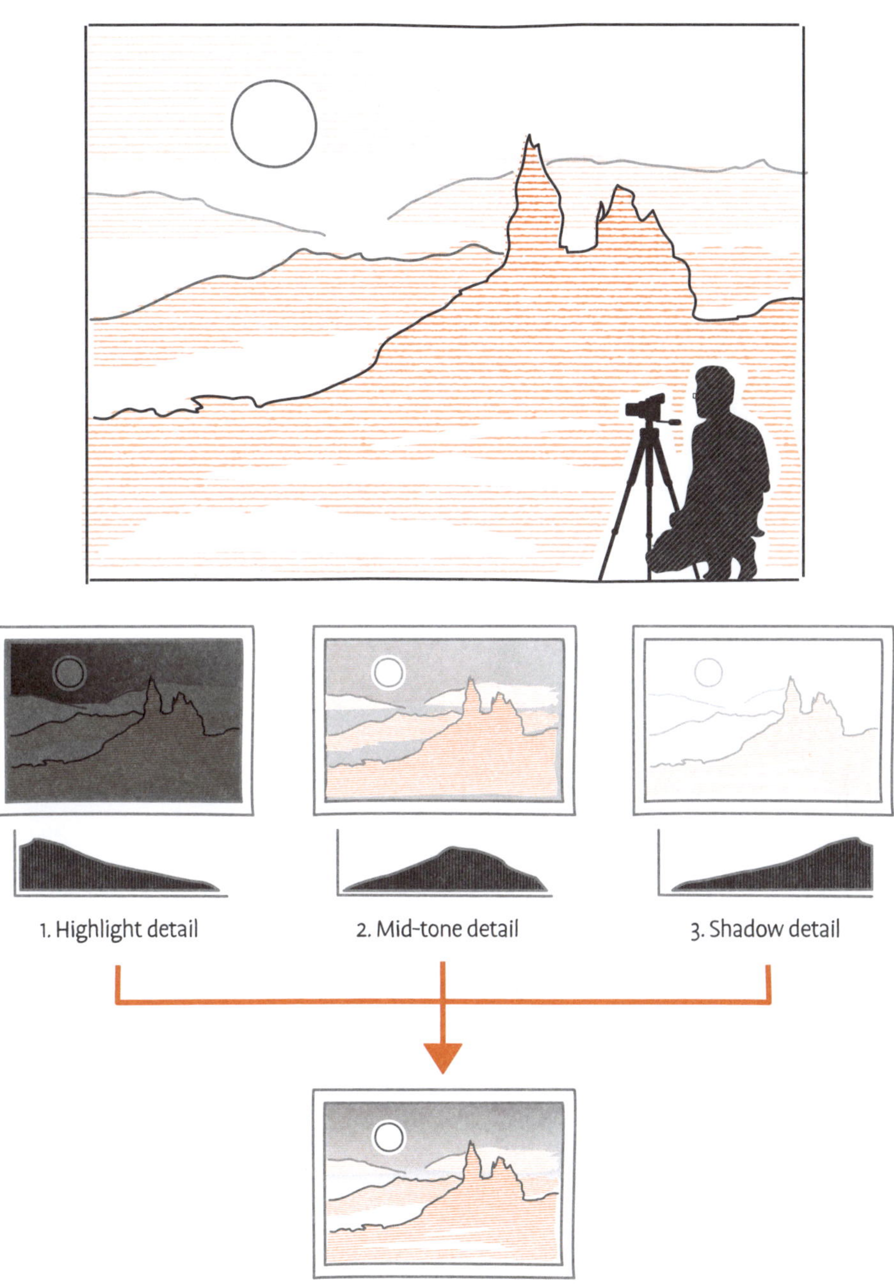

HDR image with combined exposures

Multiple exposure

What is multiple exposure?
Essentially, it's the layering of two images on top of each other. It's also known as double exposure and harks back to the days of film photography. With a film camera, two things happen when you use the film advance crank to take another picture. First, the shutter is re-cocked so it's ready to take another image, and secondly, the film is advanced, so you effectively have a blank piece of film to expose on. It is possible to disengage the film advance and just re-cock the shutter, so you're effectively taking one picture on top of another. Often, this was done in error, but some photographers did it deliberately for creative effect, and the results can be amazing, albeit with a degree of happenstance.

Some high-street portrait and wedding photographers even used the effect creatively to showcase their subjects floating in wine glasses and other kitsch delights.

Can I do this on a digital camera?
Yes! Well, probably. Most digital cameras have this as a feature, and it can be a lot of fun to play and experiment with. In fact, many cameras will allow you to layer loads of images on top of each other, in some cases up to ten or more. The camera will also take some of the exposure calculators into account too, so you don't need to worry about that.

How should I get started?
First, check your camera's manual to see how to set it up, as it'll be slightly different from camera to camera. Next, it's simply a case of experimenting and having fun, with an open mind. Start by just layering two images and seeing how they interact. Try two different types of images, for example a vase of flowers layered with a shot of some peeling paint or the sky. See how they interact and build from that.

Can't I do this in image-editing software?
Yep, you can, and it's relatively easy. Just load two images as layers in software such as Adobe Photoshop and blend the layers together. How you blend the layers can be altered using the Layer Blend mode option – typically, there are a bunch of blend modes to select from. The interaction and blending of the layers will behave differently with each blend mode and from image to image. This can be fun and a great way to unleash your creativity. However, there's nothing quite like nailing it in camera using the in-camera multi-exposure features and happenstance.

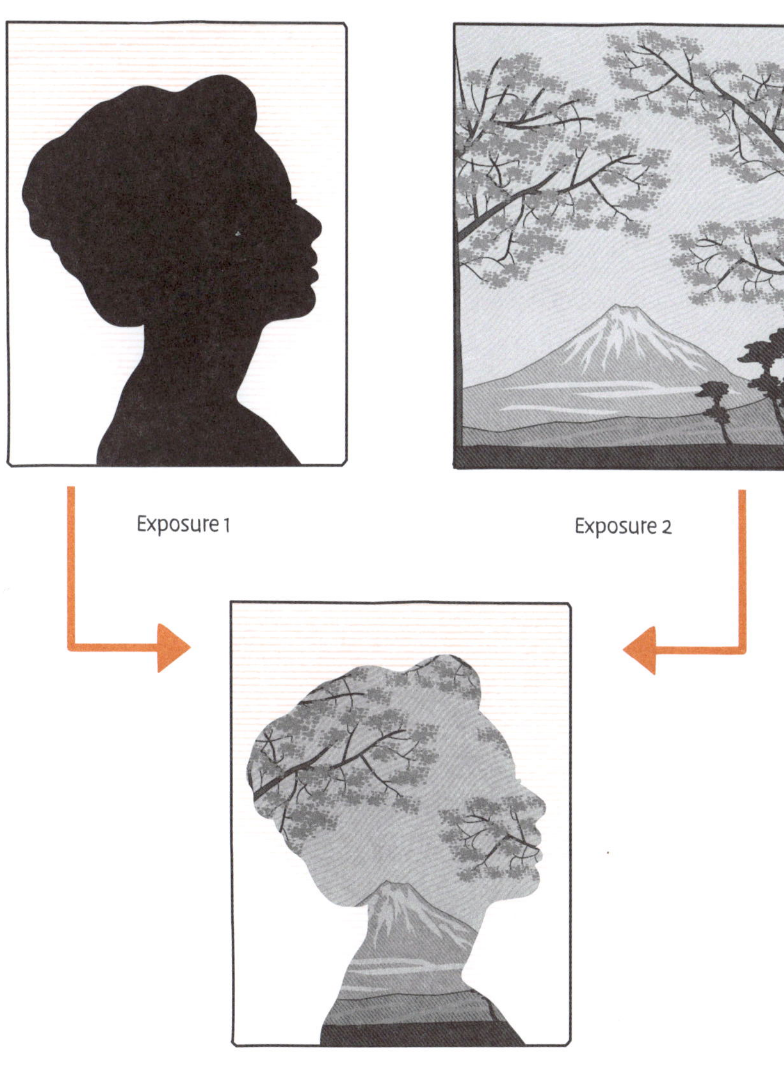
MULTIPLE EXPOSURE
Exposure 1
Exposure 2
1 + 2 = a multiple exposure

The art of ICM

What is ICM?

It's a cool, creative technique that some photographers love to use. Sometimes, a little too much! ICM stands for intentional camera movement. The general idea is to move your camera during a slow-ish exposure for impressionistic vibes. You can jiggle your camera for a funky effect or pan your camera sideways or up and down for 'streaky' abstracts.

How slow does my shutter speed need to be?

That depends on the lighting conditions and how blurry you want your image to be. A good starting point could be somewhere in the region of 1/15sec or slower. The trick is to experiment and practise. Discover what works for you and your creative vision. There is a lot of trial and error with this technique.

How do I get a slow shutter speed when it's bright?

Good question, especially as a slow shutter speed will let more light into the camera. In the first instance, ensure your ISO is as low as your camera will allow (typically, ISO 100), then look at your aperture and go small to let less light in – f/22 is ideal. If that fails and it's still too bright, you'll need to prevent light from entering by other means. This is when a neutral-density filter (ND) comes in handy. This is like putting sunglasses on the front of your lens, and it will prevent light from coming in. ND filters typically come in different densities, such as 3 stops, 5 stops and 10 stops. A 10-stop ND filter prevents so much light from getting in that you probably won't be able to see through your viewfinder to compose and focus, so do this first and then attach the filter.

What's the best way to move a camera?

The best way is the way that suits your creative vision. Ask yourself why you're using the technique and what you want the image to say. How you move the camera will create many different effects, from streaks of colour that can be calm and soothing, to jittery blurs that speak to other emotional states.

Do I need a tripod for this technique?

In some cases, especially with vertical and horizontal pans, you may want the streaks to be straight. Using the swivel mechanism of a tripod will help keep things level. If your camera isn't level, there will be a curve to the streaking lines, which some people don't like. Experiment and see what works for you.

Why do it?

It's fun and creative, and you can get some wonderfully impressionistic effects. Even if you don't like the look, it'll help you understand how changing your camera's shutter speed will affect the final picture. As is the case with lots of fancy techniques like this, use it sparingly and only when it gels with the vibe you're trying to evoke. Using fancy techniques just for the sake of it can be a shallow road to travel.

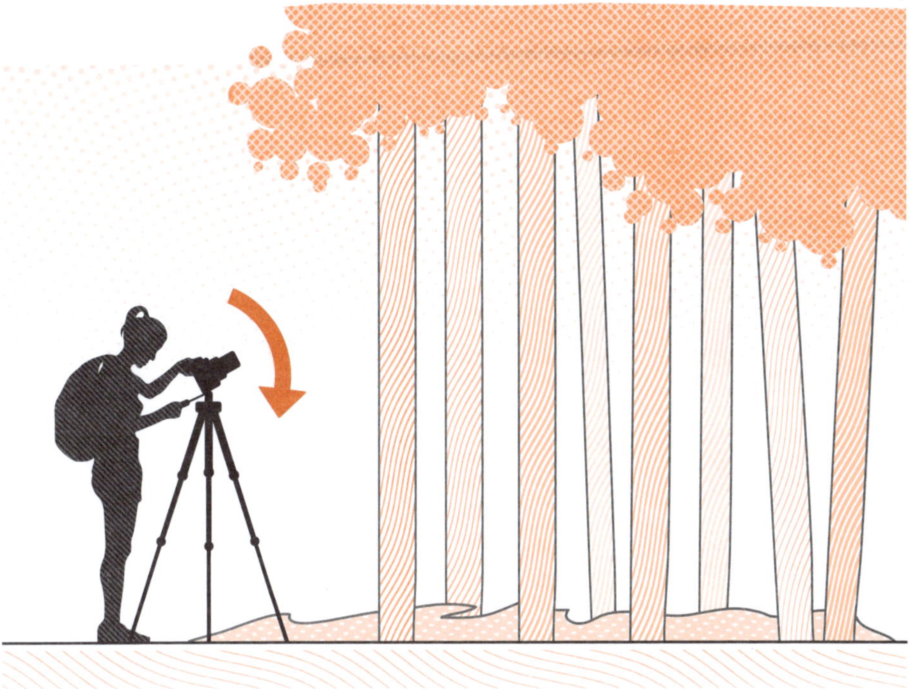

Pan your camera smoothly downwards...

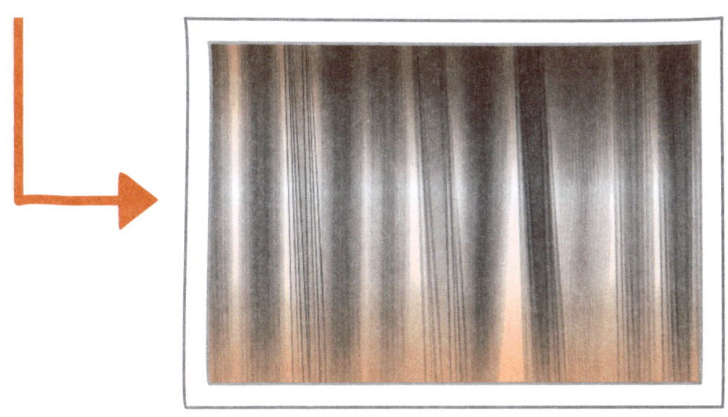

...and capture abstract vertical streaks of light

Slow exposure

I love that smooth, silky effect photographers get with water – how do I do that?
It's a great technique, which you can use to transform a landscape image into something quite magical.

Do I need any fancy kit to get started?
Yes, there is some additional kit that you'll need to consider, but it needn't be too expensive. You'll need a sturdy tripod to keep your camera steady. Exposure times can often be several seconds and sometimes even minutes long – there's no way anybody can hold a camera steady for that long without some camera shake. To avoid touching the camera when you press the shutter release – which can cause camera vibration, which can cause motion blur – use a remote trigger. Your camera's self-timer is a good alternative if you don't have one.

How slow does it need to be?
How slow depends on how smooth you want the water or clouds to appear – you'll need to experiment and decide what works with your creative vision. This is part of the creative process, and there are not necessarily right or wrong exposure times.

How do I get a slow shutter speed?
First, ensure you use your camera's lowest ISO setting (typically, ISO 100) and a small aperture such as f/22. This might prevent enough light from entering the camera to give you the slow exposure you want. It all depends on the ambient light. However, at some stage in your slow-mo journey, you'll inevitably need an ND filter (see page 34) to help achieve slow exposures.

How do I use the ND filter?
Most ND filters are in square format, and you simply attach it to the front of your camera. If you're using a dark one, such as a 10-stop, the chances are you won't be able to see through your viewfinder with it attached. In this case, you must focus and compose before attaching the filter.

And how do I calculate my long exposure with the filter attached?
It depends on which filter you use and how much light it restricts. Most manufacturers will have a table you can use to calculate the 'new' exposure. Some manufacturers make life even easier with a nifty app. After a while, you'll be able to simply calculate it in your head using your inherent knowledge and understanding of shutter speeds and exposure.

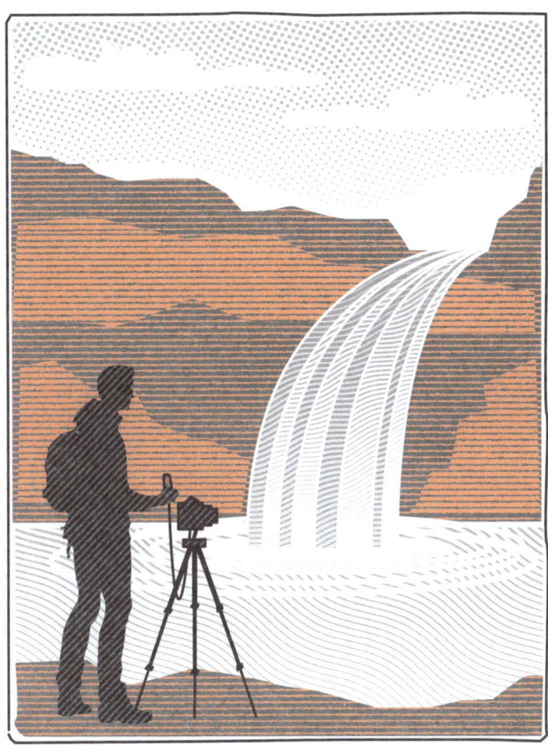

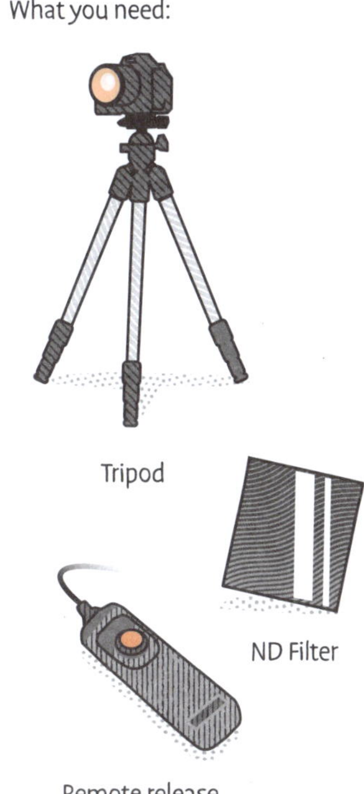

Is there anything else I should be aware of?
If you're using a DSLR camera, there's a chance that during a long exposure, the light will 'leak' through the viewfinder and cause a weird purple band across your image. Some cameras feature a little eyepiece shutter that can be activated to block stray light entering. If your camera doesn't have one, you can buy an alternative or, better still, improvise with a piece of cloth or tape.

Anything else?
Yes, not all water you come across needs to be rendered this way. The technique is cool and seductive and has terrific creative possibilities. Consequently, it can be difficult to resist using it every time you see a body of water, especially if you've just discovered the joy of the technique. The trick is to use it when it suits your creative vision and acknowledge that sometimes water looks better or suits the 'story' of your image when captured with a faster shutter speed.

Black and white

Why shoot in black and white? Isn't it a bit old-fashioned?
There are plenty of good reasons why it can be good to strip out the colour and make monochrome images. For much of photography's history, making black-and-white images was the only real option for most photographers. And even with the introduction of colour film, you were still forced to commit to black and white or colour when you bought and loaded film into your camera. With the exception of one or two very niche cameras, such as the Leica M11 Monochrom (which is eye-wateringly expensive), digital cameras capture colour images which you can then convert to black and white.

What about the black-and-white preset in my cameras?
Many digital cameras have presets and a range of film-emulation modes, and more often than not, these include some black-and-white settings. Even an iPhone has several mono presets to choose from.

But why?
Stripping away the colour is a creative decision, and some photographers love working without colour so they can concentrate on the graphical elements of the composition: the shapes, tones, textures and, of course, the light and shadow. These can look wonderful in black and white without the distraction of colour.

Which is the best way to make images black and white?
If you shoot raw files (see page 54), regardless of whether you've used a black-and-white preset, you'll need to convert your file to mono in image-editing software. Either way, image-editing software such as Adobe Lightroom, Photoshop, Affinity Photo or myriad other apps can help.

Superficially, in making an image black and white, you're simply removing the colour, however, it's significantly more nuanced than that. How you render an image with monotones has big implications on how it is 'read' by the viewer. You'll need to consider the tonal values. Are they dark or light? Is there detail in the shadow and the highlights? What about the contrast? Contrast can be hard and harsh with strong blacks and whites and fewer mid-tones, or it can be delicate and sensitive with subtle gradations of grey. Like so many aspects of photography, there is no right or wrong, just the way that plays into your creative vision and the mood you want to evoke.

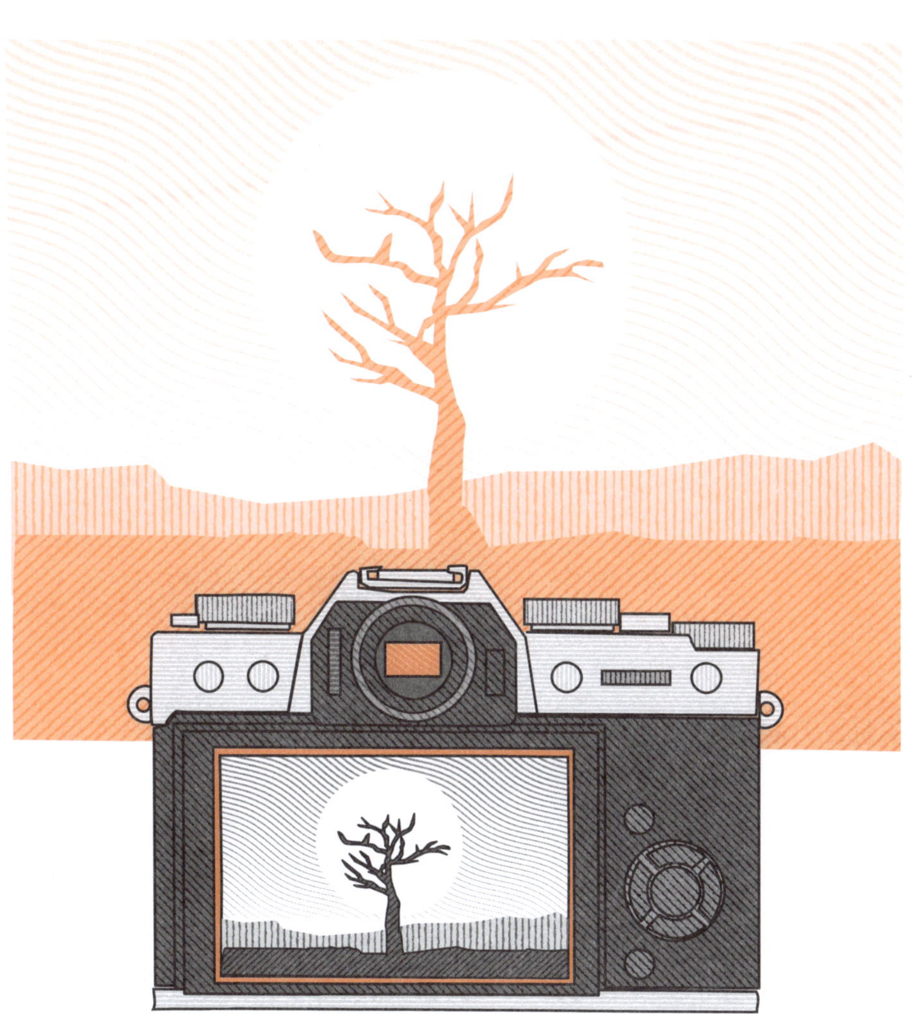

Shooting in black and white is a great way to highlight the graphic elements of your subject

Painting with light

What is painting with light?
It's a fun and creative technique that can produce some wonderful results.

How do I get started, and what do I need?
The technique works best at twilight or in the dark. The basic premise is to wander in and around your shot during a long exposure, illuminating parts of the scene with a flashlight.

How long does the exposure need to be?
The shutter needs to be open long enough for you to 'paint' with the light, so somewhere between 30 seconds and a couple of minutes. You may need to set your shutter to bulb mode. You'll need a powerful flashlight as your 'paintbrush'.

Work out your composition, looking for a scene with something to paint in the foreground, such as a characterful rock, a gnarly old tree or a dilapidated shed. Set your camera on a tripod and reduce your ISO and use a small aperture (such as f/16) to ensure you get a slow exposure. Then simply release the shutter and walk into the photo, painting the parts of it you want to illuminate with the flashlight using slow, steady movements. The longer you shine your light on an area, the lighter it will become.

But won't I be in the picture?
Technically, yes, but you'll be moving, so you won't register unless you linger too long in one spot. It also helps if you wear dark clothing and try to ensure the light doesn't shine on you.

Anything else I should be aware of?
Try to avoid pointing the torch directly into the camera's lens. Some people use an off-camera flashgun and 'pop' little flash bursts into the scene. Like most creative techniques, you need to experiment. And finally, try adding a coloured gel to the light for funky effects.

Oh, and interestingly, the French surrealist artist and photographer Man Ray is attributed as one of the first to experiment with the technique artistically in a series he made in 1935 called *Space Writing*.

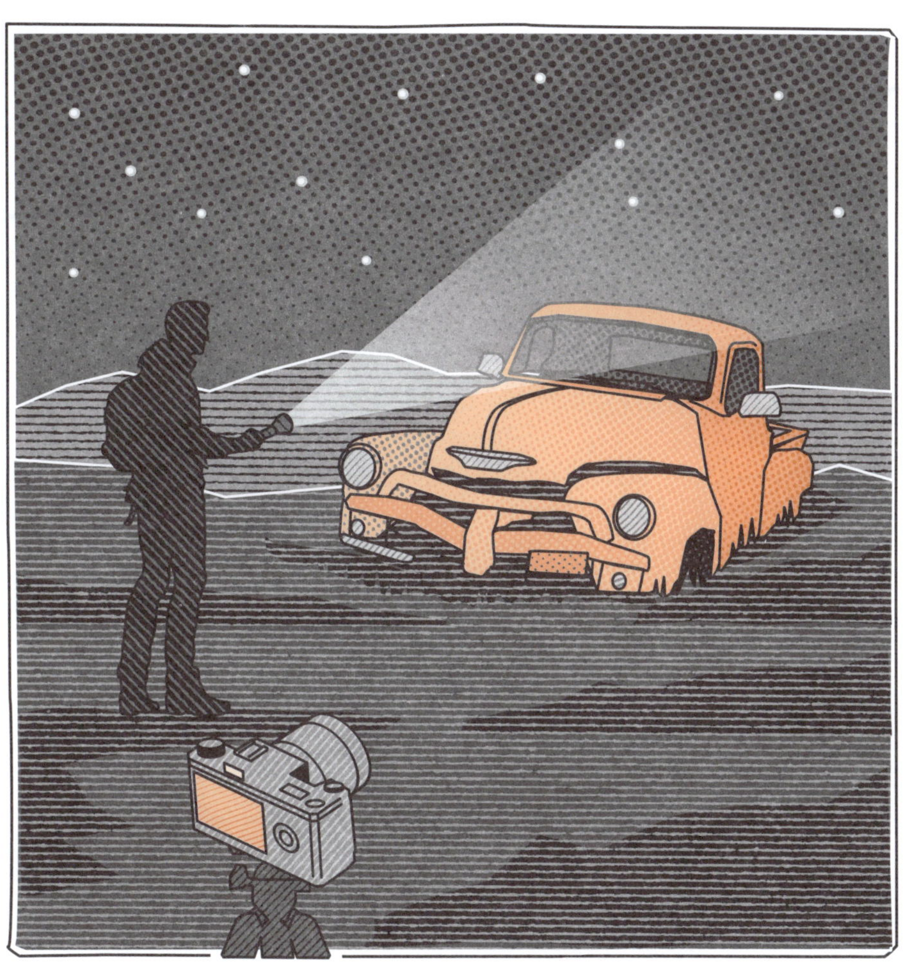

Your flashlight acts as a paintbrush during a long exposure, resulting in wonderfully atmospheric shots

High-speed drop photos

Capturing the split-second timing as water drops hit the water's surface is fun and creative. It's also not nearly as complicated as you might think.

Great, so what do I need to get started?
You'll need a camera with a macro lens, a tripod, a flashgun, a light stand with a boom arm and a couple of clamps (you can improvise and make something with common household objects), a tray to hold water and a plastic bag or valve system to release the water drops.

The setup
Look at the illustration opposite and strive to create something similar – you may need to improvise depending on what you have to hand. This can be a fun part of the creative process too. Ideally, set up in a room that's easy to make relatively dark so that ambient light doesn't interfere with the exposure.

What about camera settings?
Switch everything to manual mode, including focus. Your shutter speed must be at your camera's 'sync' speed (see page 48), typically 1/125sec or 1/250sec, as you'll be using flash. Keep your ISO low for maximum quality and your aperture at about f/11 for a decent depth of field. You'll be able to change the brightness of the exposure with your flash power. You should also set your flashgun to manual – check the manual if unsure.

How do I manually focus on a moving water drop?
Once you've established where the water drops will fall, place a marker in the water container – a pencil supported in a blob of Blu Tack is perfect. Use this as a marker to focus on and remove it, leaving your camera in manual mode – the focus point should not change.

And shoot...
Once you've established a good exposure by tweaking the flash power, just start shooting. It'll take a lot of trial and error, but in time and with a few tweaks here and there, you'll soon be getting awesome results.

Anything else I can do?
Try different coloured containers or backgrounds or even add some food colouring to the water drops. Some people use different liquids such as milk or Coca-Cola or add glycerin to alter the viscosity and, in turn, the characteristics of the drops. Some serious water-drop photographers will use special triggers and valves that release drops or sequences of drops when the shutter is released, and by fine-tuning the timing, precision drop shots can be made, but it starts getting expensive!

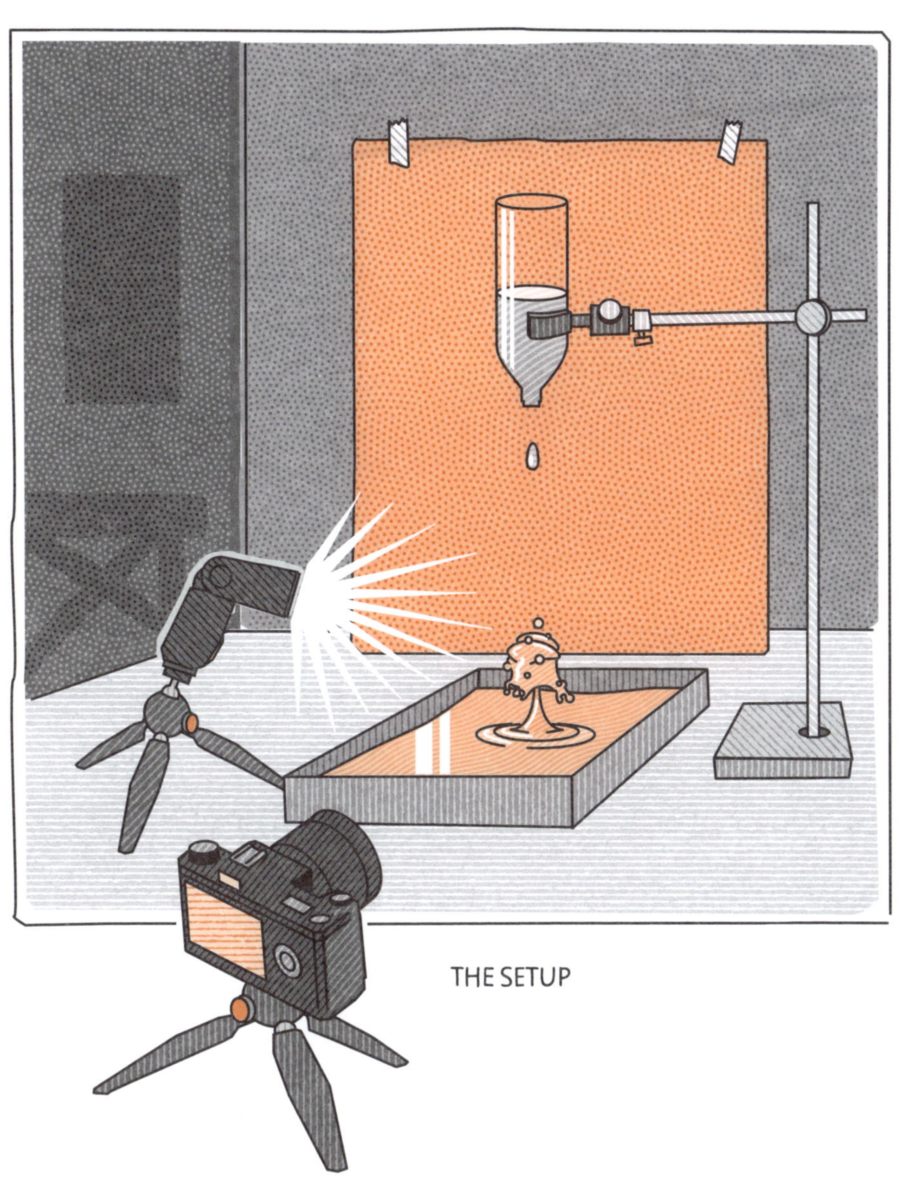

THE SETUP

Tilt-shift lenses

What is a tilt-shift lens, and why should I bother with one?

It's a specialist lens that allows you to move the angle and position of the lens independently of the sensor plane. They're quite specialist and tricky to use, however, they can be great fun once you get the hang of them. Architectural and interior photographers typically use them to eliminate the keystone (converging vertices) effect you get when pointing a camera up at a building (see page 118 for more on this and photographing buildings in general).

The tilt part of a tilt-shift lens allows you to angle the lens so it's no longer parallel to the sensor. This skews the focus in exciting ways using what's known as the Scheimpflug principle. Sounds complicated? It is. But you don't need to get too bogged down with science if that's not your thing (although it's good to drop into the conversation and impress your photographer friends – if you can pronounce it, that is!). In short, by changing the plane of focus, you can exercise even more control over your image-making. Some landscape photographers use it as another way to make a scene sharp from foreground to background, advertising photographers often use it for photographing products in a studio, and more recently, creative photographers have had fun using it to create that 'toy town' look that gives the impression of a shallow depth of field. It's fun!

Tilt-shift lenses look kind of expensive – is there a cheaper option?

To an extent, you can emulate the effects of a tilt-shift lens in image-editing software. However, while this might get you out of a pickle, it's not a very rewarding way to work. Some companies, such as Lensbaby, make super-cool lenses that effectively do the same thing as a tilt-shift lens, just less precisely, so they're not the right tools for super-slick architectural work. Still, for playing with the 'toy town' effect and creating weirdly focused and blurred images, they're great fun and more affordable.

What's 'freelensing'? Is this the same sort of thing?

I guess you could say that. It's another fun and creative technique whereby you detach your lens and hold it very close to the camera body, changing the angle and/or position slightly, much like you would with a tilt-shift lens, with the main difference being that there are no mechanical controls to hold anything in place. There's a strong chance you'll let too much light into the camera with this technique, and it's very hit-and-miss, but it can be great fun.

The most vital aspect to consider is that your lens will not be attached to your camera. As such, your camera's sensor will be very exposed and susceptible to dust and damage. Be warned and be very careful!

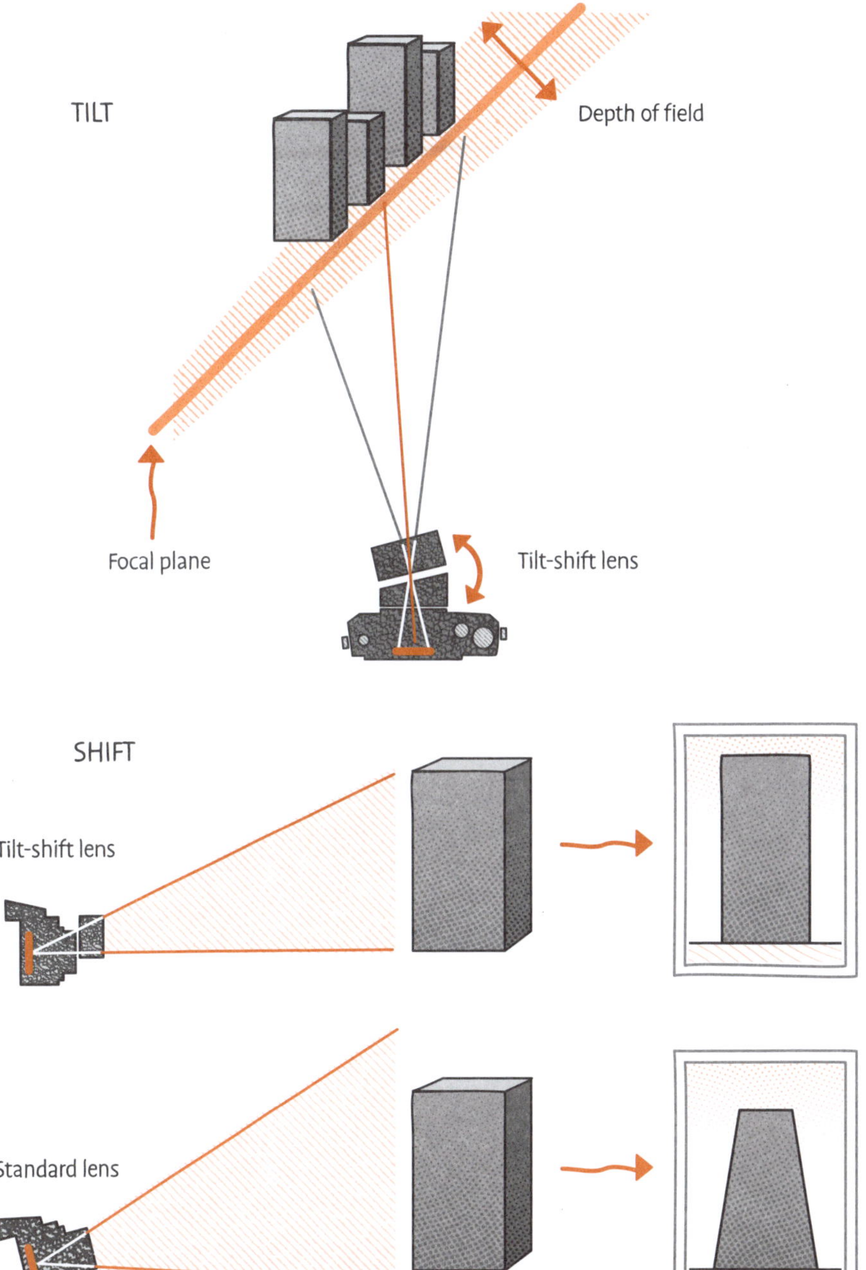
TILT
Depth of field
Focal plane
Tilt-shift lens
SHIFT
Tilt-shift lens
Standard lens

Infrared

What is infrared photography?
Infrared (IR) photography is essentially a way of expanding the type of light a normal camera's sensor, or the human eye, can see or capture. Infrared light, like X-rays and ultraviolet rays, has a frequency (measured in nanometers (nm)) that falls outside the spectrum of visible light, so it's not visible to the human eye. However, there are ways to 'see' it using specialist filters, cameras, films and techniques.

How do I do it?
There are several ways, and they all have pros and cons. Probably the easiest and cheapest way to get started is to buy a special filter, such as a relatively inexpensive Hoya R72 Infrared Filter. This blocks most visible light and only allows infrared light to pass onto your sensor. Different sensors can be more or less receptive to this, which is something to be aware of. The downside of using infrared filters is that they are nearly opaque, and very little light passes through them. This means you'll inevitably have very long exposure times. So, you'll need to use a tripod and follow the best practices discussed in slow-shutter speed photography (see page 88).

An alternative is to convert a camera specifically for IR photography. Most digital cameras have an IR-blocking filter over the sensor which can be swapped and replaced with a specialist IR pass filter, effectively turning your camera into an IR camera. As it can be fiddly and complicated to do, and hard to revert once done, the best idea is to pay a specialist company to do it. This is a great option if you've got an old camera knocking about with little value on the secondhand market but probably not something you'd want to do with a new top-of-the-range piece of kit. The main advantage of this method is that you'll be able to shoot at 'normal' exposure values and, in most instances, without a tripod or the complications of slow shutter speed photography.

Finally, you could use a film camera and purchase a specialist IR film. This is cool and ticks the hipster vibe, however, it's expensive and increasingly difficult to source.

It's also worth noting that images out of a digital camera, especially one that's been converted, might not look 'normal', and some tweaking in image-editing software will be required.

What kind of things should I photograph?
Great question! You can photograph anything you like, and, as always, it's good to experiment. However, it's worth noting that some things can look particularly cool. For example, plants, vegetation and foliage that is photosynthesizing will radiate infrared light. A tree in the height of summer will almost appear snow-covered. Many people, when they first get hold of some infrared kit, head straight to a graveyard. I guess the ghostly hues exude a gothic vibe that works. Do this, by all means, but think about pushing the creative boundaries beyond the graveyard if you can.

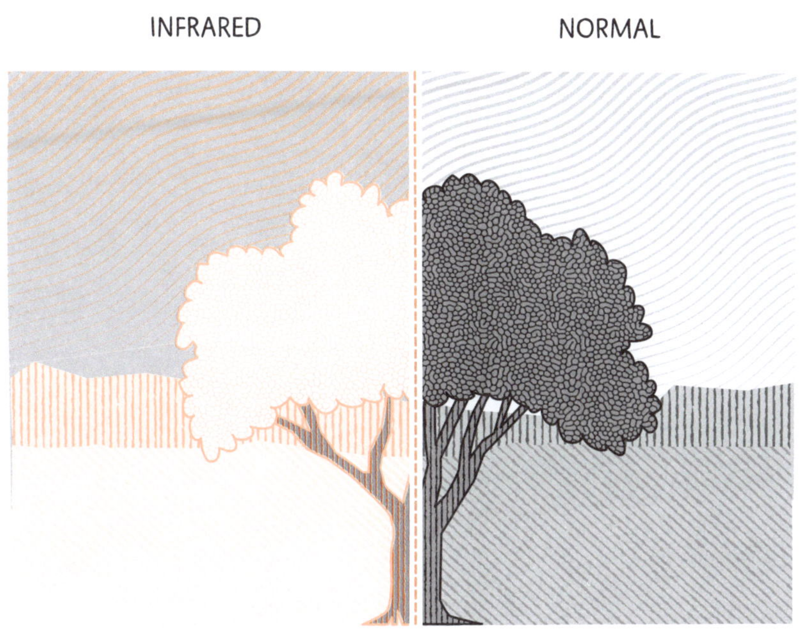
INFRARED
NORMAL

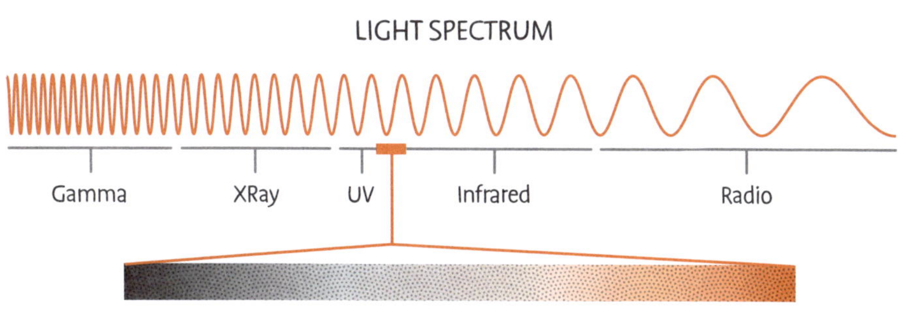
LIGHT SPECTRUM
Gamma
XRay
UV
Infrared
Radio
Visible light

Stitching panoramas

How do you make a panorama image using a regular digital camera?
It's a relatively simple, albeit fiddly, process. Sadly, it's not quite as easy as it is using a smartphone camera.

What do I need?
A tripod. With precision work like this, a tripod will help you keep everything aligned and in place. Although shooting a 'pano' without one is possible, it's not recommended. If you're super-serious, there are specialist panorama heads for tripods, but they're not necessary if you're just experimenting with the technique.

What about camera settings?
Switch to manual mode. Ideally, you need consistent exposure across all the images you intend to stitch and blend. You also want the shutter speed and depth of field to be consistent from one image to the next.

To ensure a good, consistent exposure, scan your scene and asses the lightest and darkest parts that will appear in your wide vista and select an exposure that will ensure detail in highlights and shadows.

Attach your camera in the vertical (portrait) orientation. This will maximize the resolution of the final image.

How do I shoot it?
Once you've established the exposure, take a series of shots starting from the left. Crucially, you need to overlap each image by about a third. Activating the grid view on your camera's viewfinder can help with this. Ideally, you want to pivot around the lens, and some speciality tripod heads can help with this. However, in practice, it doesn't matter – unless you're going pro!

Now what?
In your image-editing software, you simply blend the images, and hey presto, you have a stunning panorama. Check your software to see how this is done. Typically, it's a relatively painless automatic process, although you may need to correct the final crop, remove a little distortion and tweak the tones and colours.

Anything else?
If you want to get fancy, geek out and get super-accurate with panoramas, use a tilt-shift lens (see page 96) and take three shots, extending as far left and right as possible and combining the multiple shots. For ultimate accuracy, keep the lens static and shift the camera body.

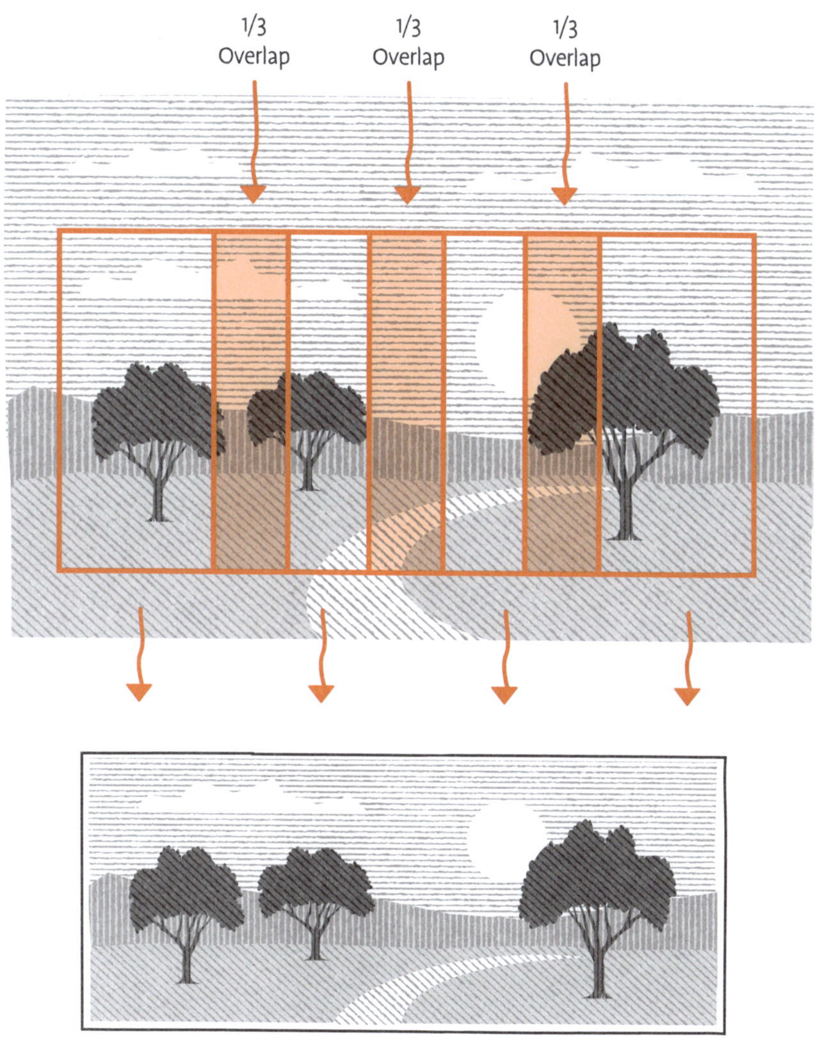

Stitched panoramic

Hockney-style joiners

What is a Hockney-style joiner?

A Hockney-style joiner is a fun and creative way to explore space and perspective. The approach is inspired by the work of British artist David Hockney (b.1937). In the 1980s, Hockey made a series of photo collages by photographing a scene from slightly different angles and distances. He then stuck the images together to make the bigger picture, called joiners. Initially, he made a collage by assembling square Polaroid photos in quite formal grids but later used prints made in a photo lab and stuck them, sometimes overlapping, onto a bigger canvas.

How do I do that with a digital camera?

Pick a subject and take a bunch of photos at slightly different angles but broadly from the same position. This doesn't need to be a precision exercise like stitching a panorama (see page 100), so being a little haphazard adds to the aesthetic, and throwing a little happenstance into the creative mix can often present interesting results that you might not have otherwise considered.

What subjects work best?

Hockney has great examples of portraits, simple domestic spaces and wider landscapes. Start small to get a sense of the technique and grow from there.

Can I 'arrange' the images on my computer?

You can do whatever you want – that's the joy of creativity. So, yes, import the images into one big document on your computer and use the Move tool to place them onto the 'canvas'. You could even try overlapping some images and changing the layer blending mode to see how they overlap. Unleash your creativity and go wild.

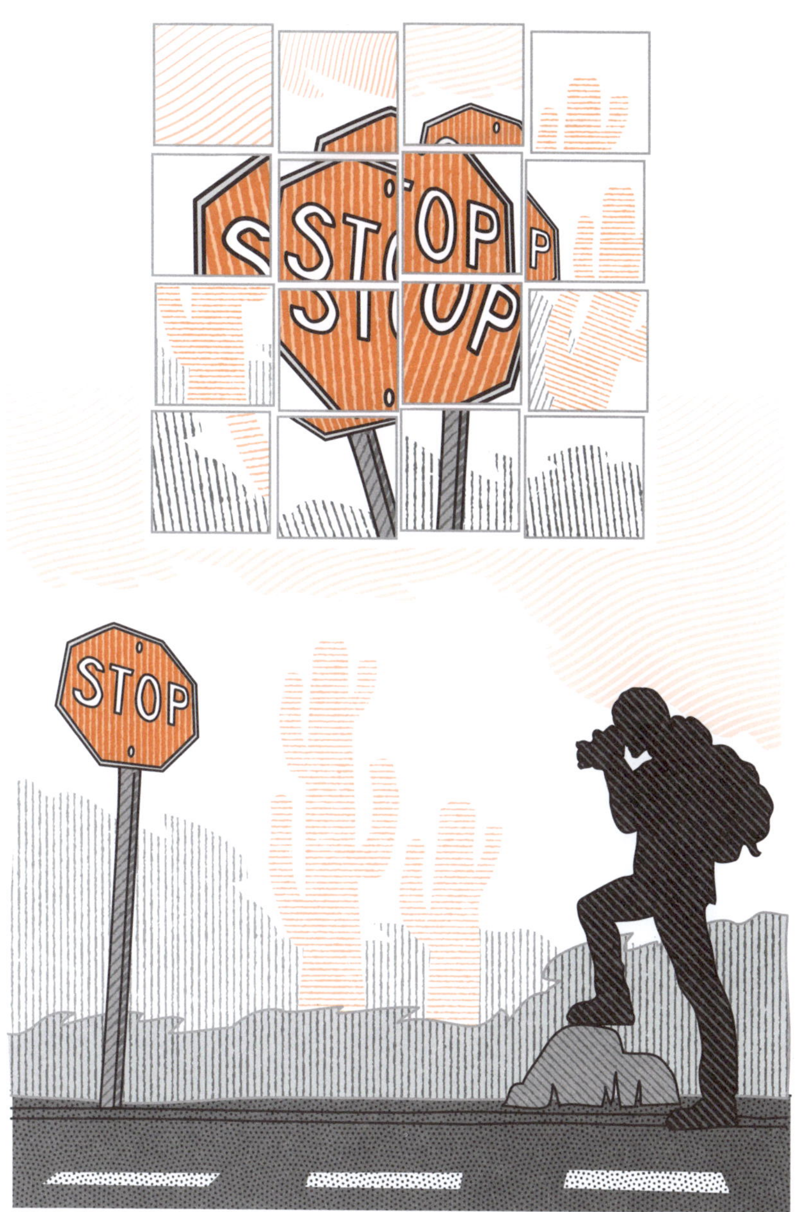
STOP

Refractions and distortion

Refraction is the bending of light and is a fantastic way to incorporate some science into your creativity. As light passes through transparent substances such as air, water and glass, it bends and even changes direction. It can all get a bit scientific, but all we need to know is that we can have fun with our creative potential.

How do I get creative and bend some light?
Refraction occurs when light passes from one medium through another, so start with air and water. Place a glass half filled with water on the table and create a white backdrop using a sheet of white card. Set up your camera, ideally on a tripod, and place a pencil or something similar in the glass and notice how it changes angle when it meets the water. This is refraction. You'll probably start seeing examples of it everywhere now that your eyes are attuned to it.

Next, print out a background with diagonal stripes and see what happens when you place it behind the glass. Introduce multiple glasses and go crazy.

The 'classic' example of this technique typically features a wine glass with a background of two colours, halved in the middle. The glass is placed directly in the middle of the backdrop, and the colours switch where the glass is.

Does anything else work?
Water droplets can be fun too. Spray them onto a sheet of glass, place an object behind the glass and be amazed when you see your object appear upside down and back to front in all the little droplets.

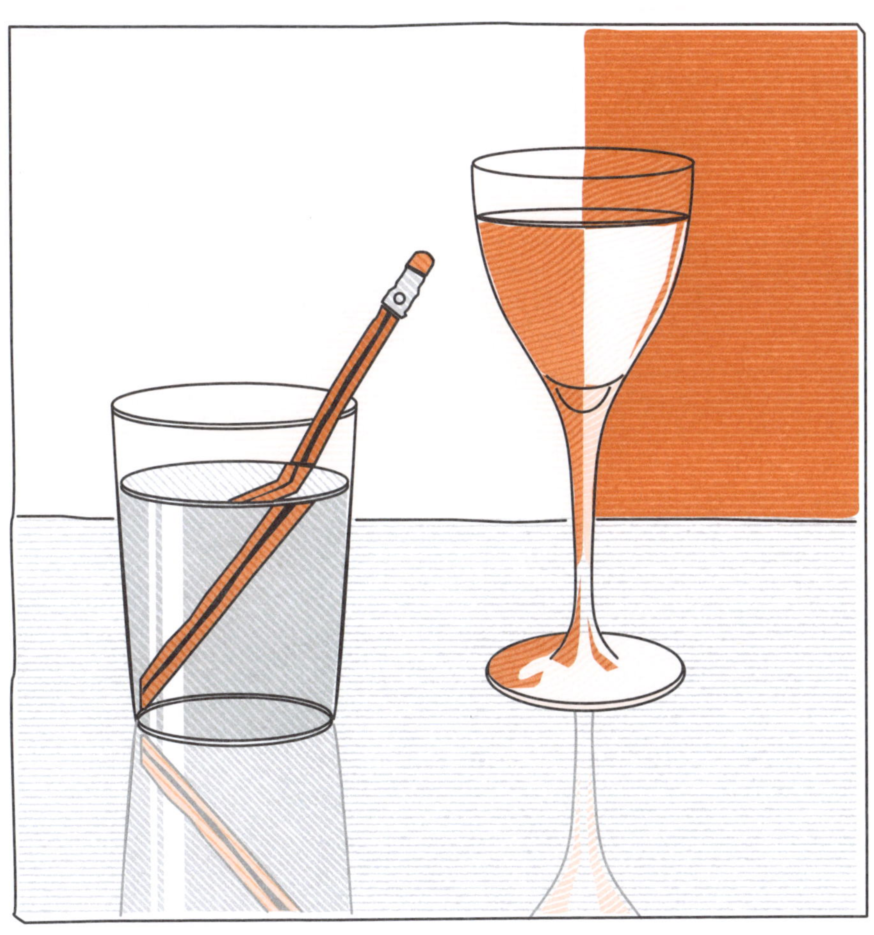

A classic example of the technique, featuring a wine glass split straight down the middle in front of a two-colour background

Storytelling

Have you ever thought of photography as a language and a way to tell stories?

Not really, but I'm intrigued, tell me more.
There's a lot to cover on this subject, and storytelling using the language of photography is as complex and nuanced as the art of storytelling with written words. In the first instance, take a look around you and reflect on how photography has been used to communicate to you throughout the day, from a story in the newspaper, a photo in a cookbook or the record of a family event posted on social media, to the advertisements you see on your commute to work and everything in between. The language of photography is always being used to tell you something, show you something or sell you something.

I hadn't thought of photography like that – how's that useful to me and my photography?
It's useful to take a moment to think about what you want to say and communicate through photography. This will help inform how you grow creatively. You may feel like the photographic equivalent of a poet or maybe a journalist; both are equally valid and use visual language as an expressive tool.

How should I start?
Start by looking at the work of other photographers and see what resonates with you and ask yourself why. Use this as a springboard for further enquiry.

In more practical terms, what can I do?
Start by trying to tell the story of something simple such as preparing a meal. Initially, do this as a series of documentary-style photographs. Make a sequence of four shots that tell the story – think of an establishing shot using a wide-angle lens, add some supporting mid-range shots and a detail or two, and put them together to produce a mini photo essay. Maybe this makes you feel a little creatively unsatisfied. If so, focus on how you 'feel' about cooking and, using the techniques in this book, find ways to express this feeling photographically.

SIMPLE FOUR-SHOT PHOTO STORY

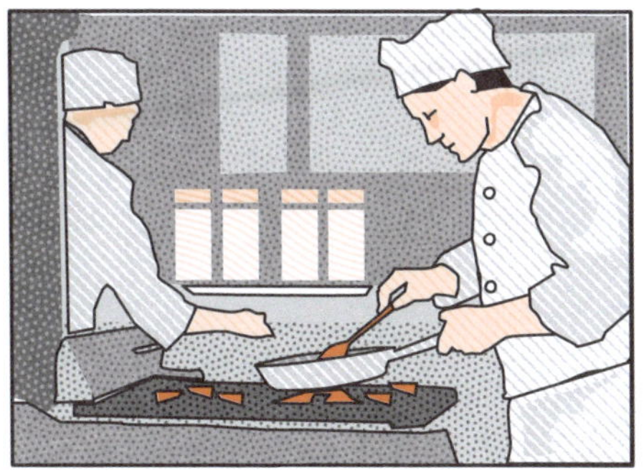

Opening establishing shot

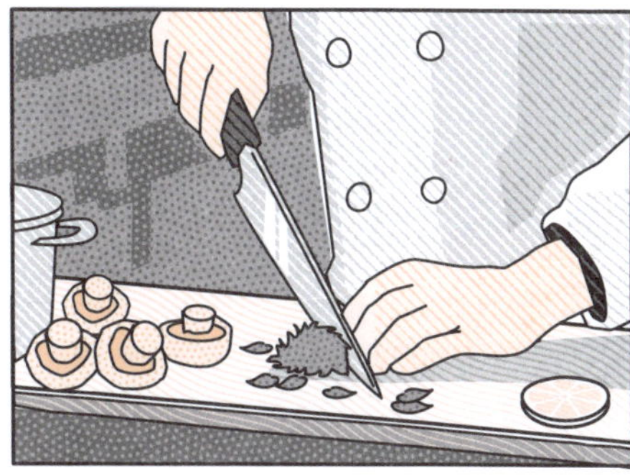

Detail

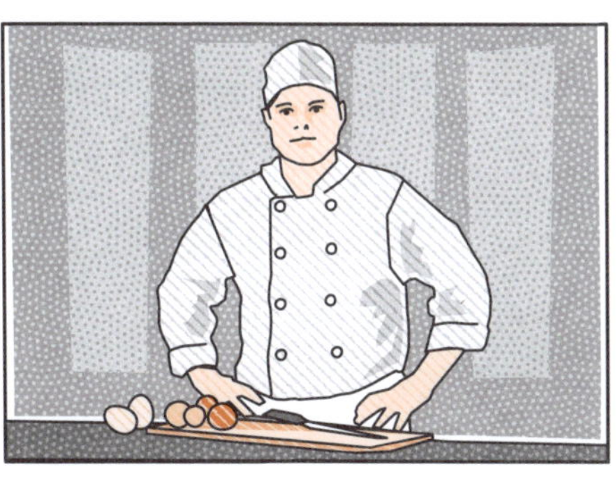

Portrait

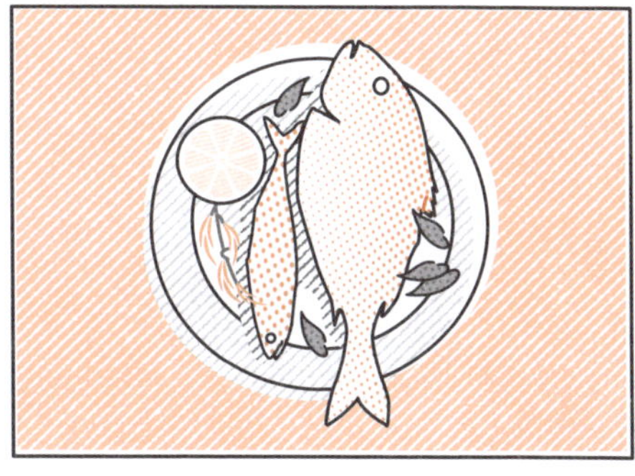

The finished product

Looking for abstracts

What is abstract photography?

Like abstract art, abstract photography is not concerned with attempting to make images that represent recognizable objects or scenes. Instead, images are more concerned with shape, tone, line, colour, form and texture, which can in turn be used to express the creator's feelings about the world. However, unlike abstract painting, photography presents an interesting conundrum: it essentially records stuff from the real world as we point our camera at it. So, making abstract images with a camera requires a keen eye and is more complex than many assume.

How do I start?

A great way to start is to simply walk with your camera with an open eye and mind. Typically, abstract images can present themselves in the more banal corners of the world: the peeling paint on the wall of a decrepit building or the rusty marks on the side of a skip can be a treasure trove of opportunities. In the first instance, look for colours, shapes and textures, and frame them so that they're removed from their context; it shouldn't be immediately obvious what the image is of. Once you open your eyes and look, you'll see potential abstracts everywhere. After a while, step back and think about 'seeing' abstracts in a wider view.

What about camera settings?

Technically, you can keep your 'abstract' photography simple, as it's more about looking and seeing than applying fancy techniques. That said, you always need to be mindful of image quality, especially if you want to make large fine art prints. Strong, bold shadows can work well in your abstract armoury and, as such, can be an interesting subject to shoot in the midday sun, a time when most photographers hang up their cameras and wait for the subtle rays of the golden hour.

Some of the techniques discussed in this book also lend themselves well to abstract photography: intentional camera movement (see page 86), multiple exposures (page 84) and slow exposures (page 88).

Anything I should check out for inspiration?

Look at abstract painting as well as photography. There is a rich history of abstract painting that you'll quickly find online. For further research and some interesting photographers working in this field, start with Ellen Carey and Aaron Siskind.

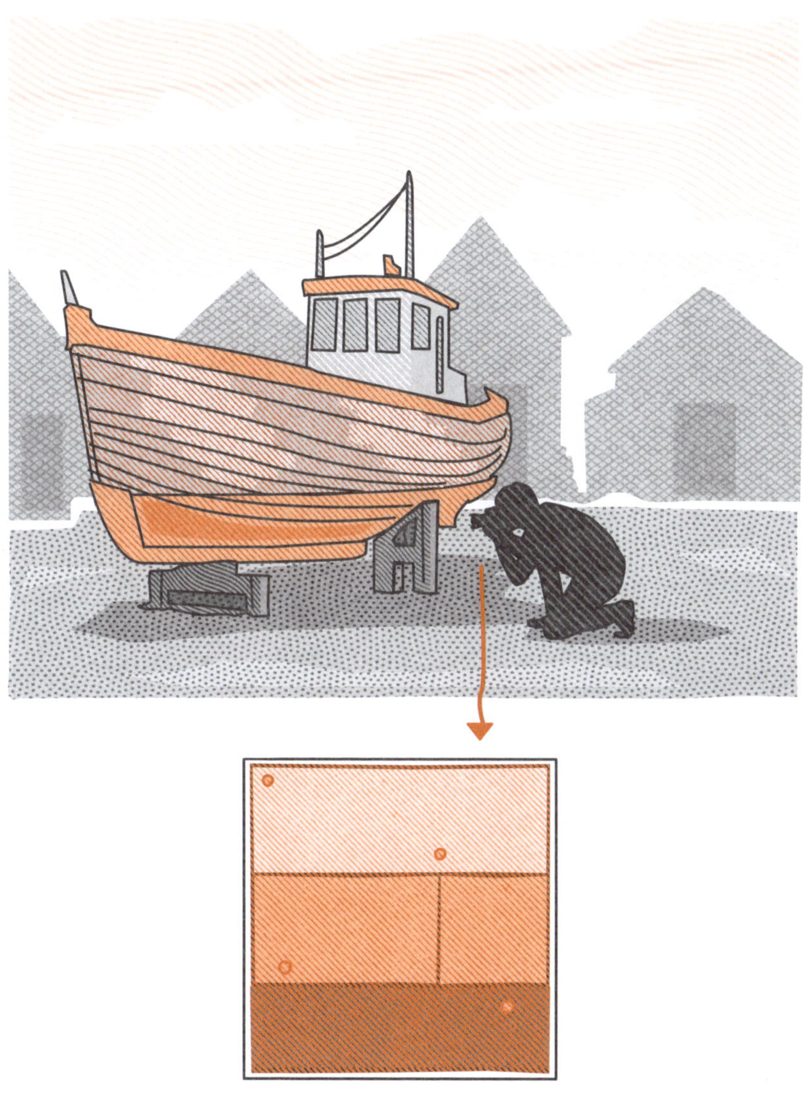

Abstract detail

On being minimal

What is minimal photography?
It's a way of seeing that strives to simplify a scene into as few essential elements as possible. Minimalist photographers seek ways to strip down a composition to its barest form, often characterized by the simple use of clean lines, bold shapes and an acute awareness of negative space.

How do I get started?
In the first instance, look at examples of minimalist photographers and study their work. A simple online search will throw up many fine examples, but the Japanese photographer Hiroshi Sugimoto or US-based British photographer Michael Kenna are good places to start.

Go to a location and spend some time contemplating it. Look for angles and take the time to notice and acknowledge how the light is falling, how shadows are being cast and so on. Look at the textures, the colours and, of course, the negative space. Move around a space and seek out ways to simplify the scene into as few elements as possible. Regardless of whether you like this kind of photography, it's still a good exercise to try, and it'll help with your composition and will refine the way you see.

Should this be colour or black and white?
There is no right or wrong. Stripping away the colour and looking in black and white is a good way to simplify a scene, focusing on shape, line, tone, texture and light, but working in mono alone won't make you a minimalist. Colour can be a wonderful tool too. Look for bold, solid complementary colours or gentle, harmonious colours.

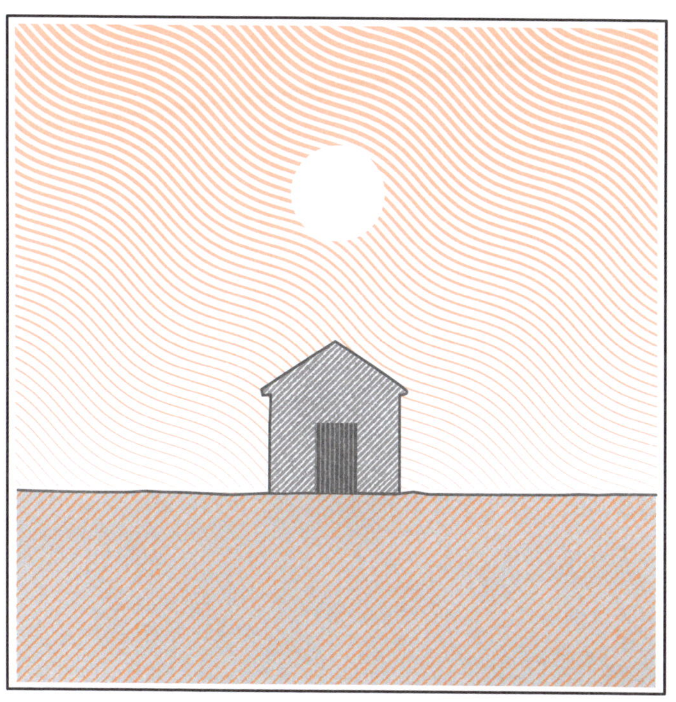

Minimal landscapes – keep it simple!

Finding your creative mojo

All these techniques are cool and creative, but sometimes I just don't know what to photograph.
You're not alone! Finding your creative mojo can be a challenge. Walking out of your front door on a mission to make photos is just the first step. What you decide to photograph is another question altogether. However, there are a bunch of tools and exercises that you can use to help get your creative juices flowing.

Great, what are they?
While it may sound counter-intuitive, creating boundaries, enforcing deadlines and making yourself accountable can all feed into the creative process.

That doesn't sound much like fun!
It doesn't, but stick with it. Here's an exercise that'll enforce boundaries, stimulate creativity and help you get going when you walk out the front door and find yourself in a conundrum as to what to photograph. Select one lens or focal length, say 50mm, decide on a route and take a timer or stopwatch. Set your timer to five minutes and follow your predetermined route. When the timer goes off, stop, look and react photographically to wherever you happen to be. Sometimes, you might luck out and stop next to something inherently photogenic, but at other times, you may find yourself challenged with making an interesting photograph from a garbage can. By the end of a two-hour walk, you'll have made 24 images. Try editing this into a coherent body of work. Do this regularly along different routes and you'll flex your creative muscles and use boundaries to exercise your looking, seeing and process. This will make you a better photographer, guaranteed.

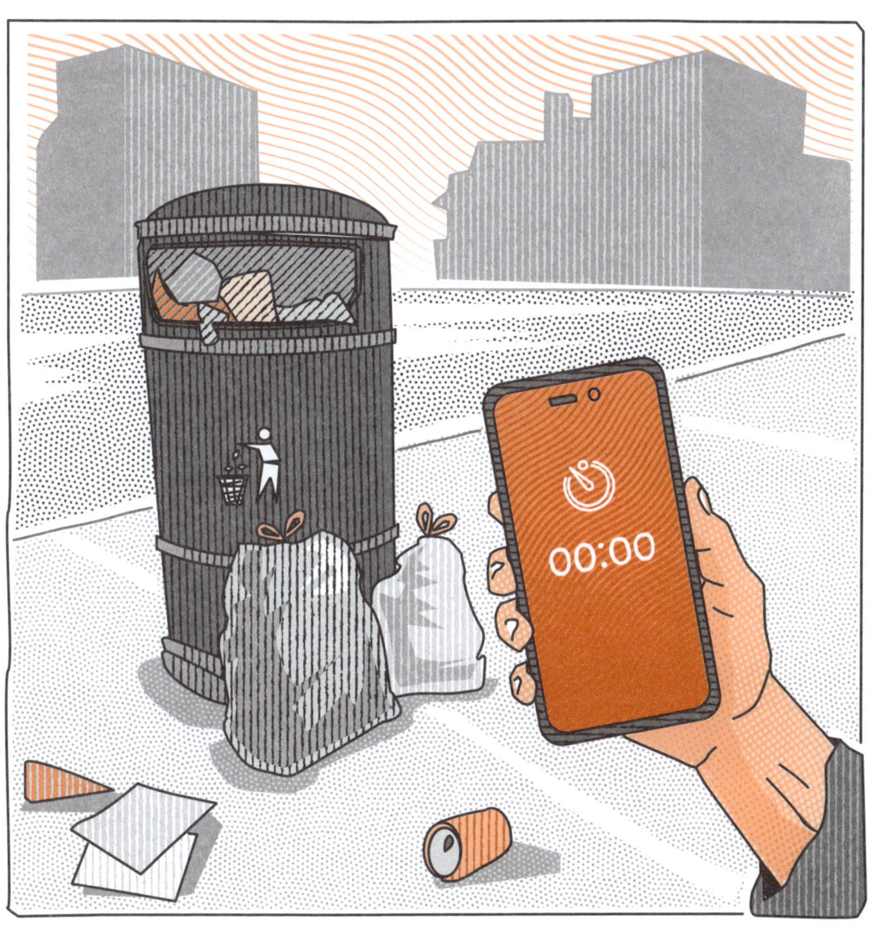

When the timer goes off, it's time to get your shot!

Creative techniques: Recap

In this chapter, we've explored some core techniques and ways to expand your creative repertoire. They all require plenty of practice to perfect, so try not to get too frustrated if at first you don't succeed. Once mastered, you will have added these techniques to your 'creative toolbox', so that you can call on them whenever needed.

Five top tips

1 Practise, practise and practise. Some of the skills highlighted in this chapter are tricky to master; learn from your mistakes, and stick with it. You'll get there if you do. I promise.

2 Have a go at all of the techniques, even if it's not something you think you'll be interested in. You never know where the creative path might take you, and you'll be growing your skill set.

3 While specialist kit might help with some of these techniques, it's rarely vital. In the first instance, improvise and experiment.

4 Look for like-minded people to share your photographic journey. Not only can this be a great way to grow creatively, you may also have fun and make new friends.

5 Creativity is like exercise: the more you do it, the easier it becomes. Try and develop a habit of photographing everyday, even if it's just with your phone.

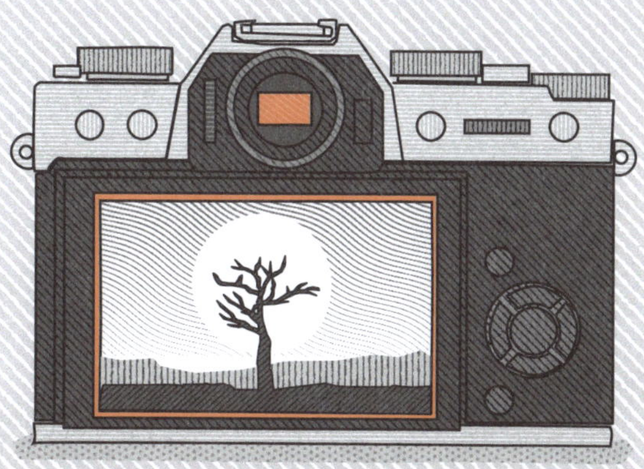

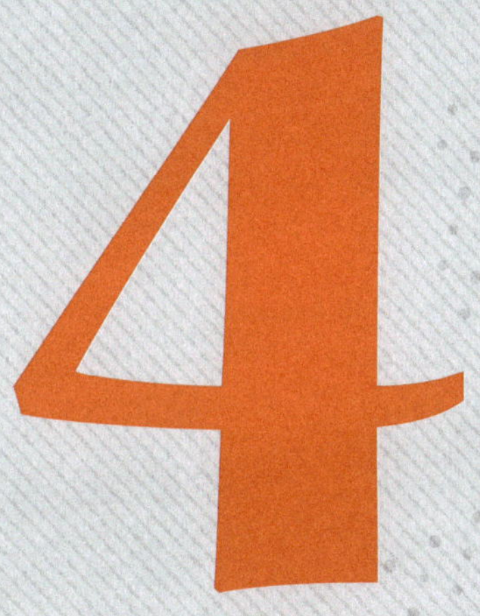

HOW TO PHOTOGRAPH

How to photograph: Buildings

What's the best way to photograph a building?

Architectural and interior photography is an art in its own right and some photographers work exclusively in it. It's a specialist genre, as there are a whole bunch of challenges to consider. That said, the best way to photograph a building is in the way that you respond to it creatively. However, if you're a stickler for convention, some aspects to shooting buildings are generally considered important, mainly to do with perspective and specifically trying to keep verticals vertical and horizontals horizontal.

Why are verticals important, and what is this 'keystoning' I've heard about?

Keystone is effectively a perspective distortion created when your camera is not levelled. If you've ever stood underneath a building and pointed your camera up, you'll notice the vertical lines converge and it appears as if the building is leaning backwards. Architectural photographers don't like this. The solution is simple: you need to position your camera so that its sensor is 90 degrees to the subject, and all vertical lines will appear straight.

How do I do that?

That's where it becomes complicated. Ideally, you would simply use a long lens, go a long way from the building, find an elevated position, make sure everything's level, straight and perpendicular, and take the shot. Easy, right? Of course not, and very rarely is this possible. This is why most photographers specializing in photographing buildings will use a tilt-shift lens.

What's a tilt-shift lens, and do I really need one?

It's a specialist lens that allows parts of the lens to be moved up and down by twisting a knob without moving the camera (see page 96). Effectively, being able to 'shift' the image that falls on your camera's sensor means you don't need to angle your camera up. The camera's sensor can remain perpendicular to the building, and your final image will not show converging verticals. The tilt bit of a tilt-shift lens changes the angle of the lens and is more useful for shifting planes of focus. This can be fun too. By the way, you'll have to focus these lenses manually.

What if I don't have a tilt-shift lens?

If you want to experiment, try renting one for a weekend and see how you get on. If you don't have access to a lens, it is possible to correct the perspective in most image-editing software, saving a lot of hassle in the field. If you plan on doing this, shoot a little wider than you envisage your final image being, as the correction process will crop into the image. Try and use it for fine tweaking rather than salvaging an image.

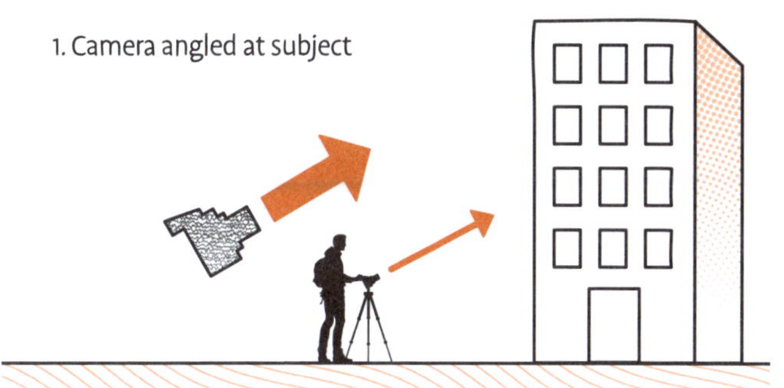

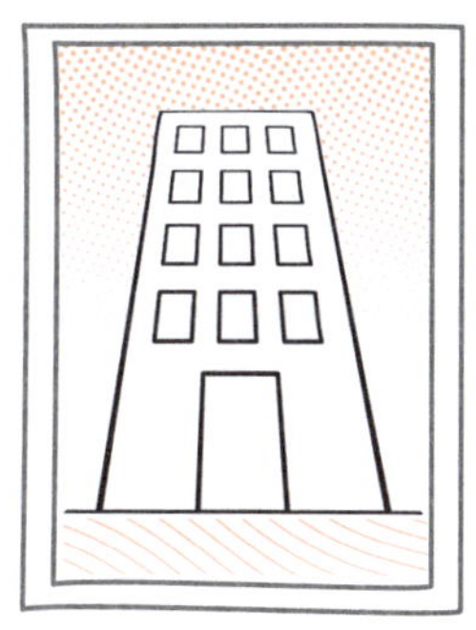

Image distorted

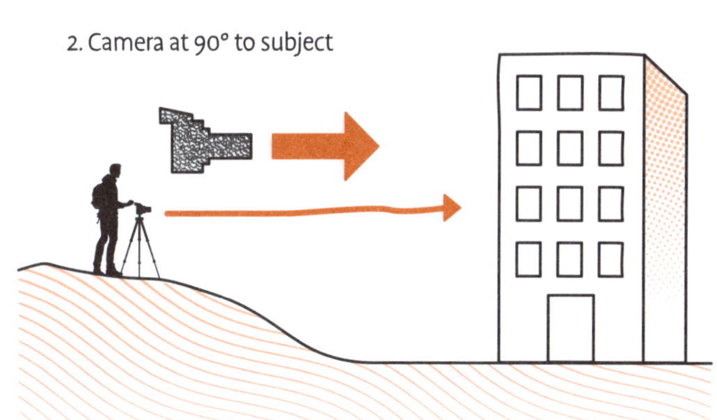

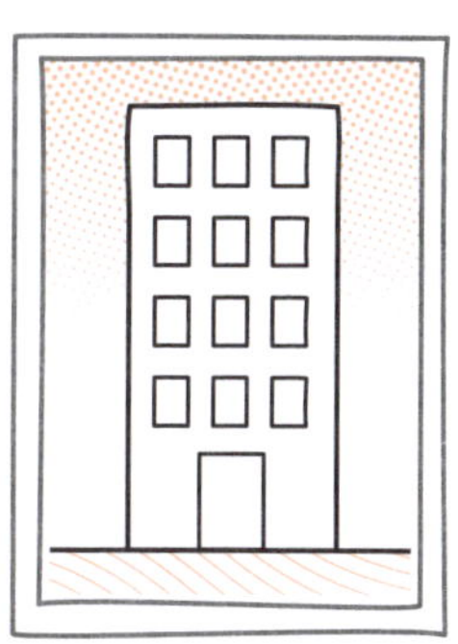

Verticals straight

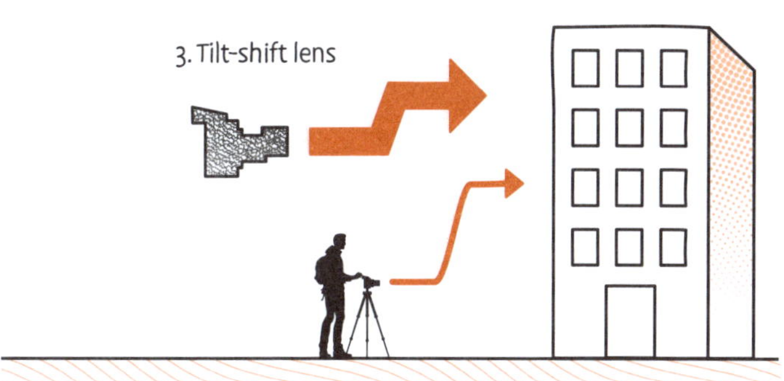

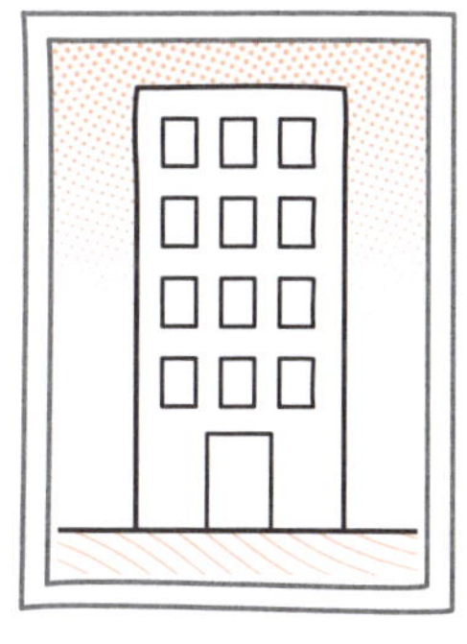

Verticals straight

How to photograph: The 'everyday'

What do you mean by photographing the 'everyday'?

Photographing everyday scenes, whether it's a still life in your kitchen sink, the light falling in a particular way in your bathroom, the colourful characters en route to the grocery store or the strange way a vine creeps across a garage. These seemingly ordinary vignettes can all become epically poetic if seen, appreciated and photographed sympathetically. Take the time to notice, see and acknowledge these moments and scenes with your camera, mindfully and appreciatively.

But why should I do that? I don't necessarily want to photograph the kitchen sink...

There are many reasons, not least that it'll help you grow as a photographer. When new to photography, some people get hung up on the idea that it's all about capturing epic vistas at unique locations in the perfect light and weather conditions. While this can be fun and rewarding, it can also be limiting, as this type of photography tends to be 'by appointment'. It requires time, effort and probably some expense to ensure you're in the right location at the right time.

The best way to learn photography, or any new skill, is to practise and practise some more. Limiting yourself to these honeypot locations also limits the amount of practice you put into your photography. By embracing 'everyday' and thinking about that as your subject, you'll be learning to look and, most importantly, see all the time. You'll also be handling your equipment repeatedly, becoming more familiar with its knobs, buttons, dials, menu features and ergonomics. You'll be learning to see how your camera sees, honing your camera vision.

Practice is good, but what's this got to do with creativity?

Photography is an art form. As such, it is deeply subjective, and people make photographs for different reasons. However, besides practising and honing your skills, exploring the everyday and finding beauty in the mundane will encourage you to see and develop a deeper appreciation of the world. To many, this can become a wonderful way to tell stories and comment on the world using the language of photography. If you're not so enamoured by the beauty of the kitchen sink, it'll still help you learn to look at and appreciate your environment and surroundings so that you can make more engaging and personal images when you finally get to an epic landscape.

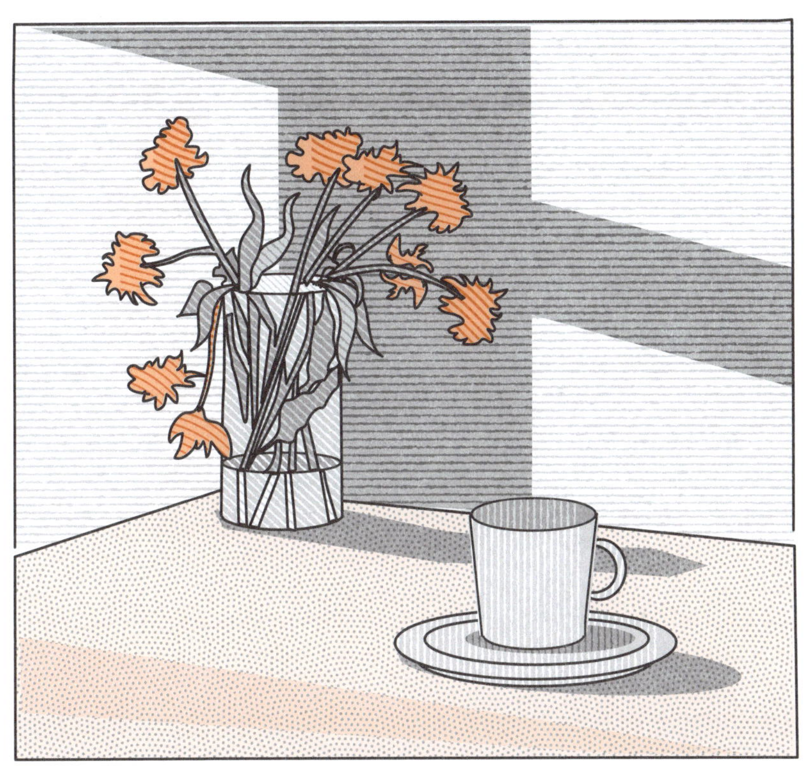

Train your eye to find photographic
opportunities in any setting

How to photograph: People

How do you start photographing people?
There are many ways to photograph your fellow human beings, from corporate headshots and family snaps to fashion shoots and documentary-style encounters. You can even turn your camera on yourself and make self-portraits. So, where to get started largely depends on what you want to photograph and how. Over the next few pages, we'll examine different approaches to the subject.

What kit should I use?
That also depends on who you're photographing and why. However, a couple of things are worth considering as a general guide. Firstly, be very familiar with your camera and kit. There's nothing more likely to ruin the moment than your subject getting bored or irritated as you scroll through menus or fiddle with settings. So, get everything sorted beforehand and take some practice shots before a session starts. Typically, portrait photographers use longer focal lengths such as 85mm or 110mm (35mm equivalent). These short telephoto focal lengths are generally more flattering to a subject's face than a wide-angled lens. See what a difference two focal lengths make to the facial features.

Do I need fancy lights and reflectors and so on?
No, you don't need them to make a decent portrait, however, being aware of the light and how it will affect your portrait is vital. Photographers will often use artificial studio lights if they're working in a studio. They give you complete control but also potentially add layers of complexity and cost. In the first instance, work with natural light and perhaps a reflector, diffuser or other light modifiers for extra control. Turn the page, and we'll look at a basic studio set-up for portraiture. In the meantime, experiment with natural light. Find a willing and patient subject to experiment with and bribe them with coffee and cake if necessary. Go for a walk and photograph them in different lighting conditions: try the open shade of a doorway, the light from a north-facing window, the high-contrast light of the midday sun or the dappled light underneath a tree. Some types of light will work better than others, so build this knowledge into your creative repertoire.

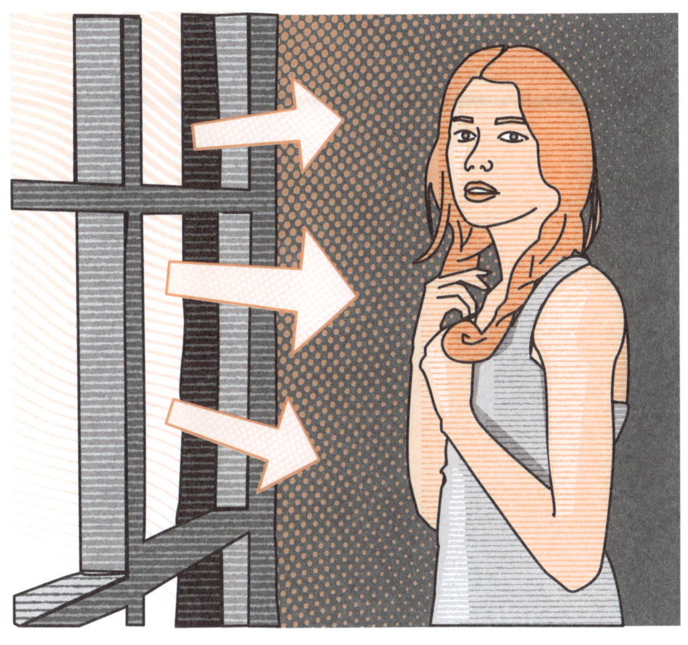

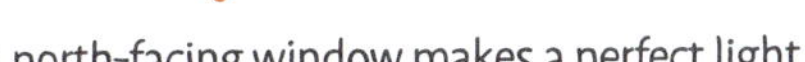

A north-facing window makes a perfect light source

Why should I use a studio for portraiture?
You don't have to use a studio. However, some types of portraiture are better suited to working in a controlled studio environment where you can use lights, backgrounds and other accessories for complete creative control. Subjects such as fashion, beauty, corporate and actor headshots lend themselves well to studios.

What do I need to get started?
It can start to get expensive quickly, as you'll need lights, light stands and modifiers, backdrops, and so on. There are a bunch of relatively inexpensive starter studio kits on the market. You'll also need space, although you can easily adapt a living room. In the first instance, it might be worth renting a studio or attending a workshop to see if this is the kind of photography you want to do before spending your hard-earned dosh.

Should I use flash or LED lights?
There are pros and cons to both. LED lights have become much better in recent years and have the advantage that you can see the effect the light has on your subject. Regardless of what you use, the principles of lighting remain broadly the same.

And what are the basic principles?
Convention suggests that using two or three lights is a good starting point. These will comprise a key light, a fill light and a backlight. Look at the diagram to get a sense of the position of the lights. There are endless possibilities as your skill, confidence and creativity grow and flourish.

The basic idea is that the key light creates a sense of direction and is typically positioned at a 45-degree angle to the subject and pointing down from a slightly higher viewpoint. The fill light is positioned opposite the key light and, usually from a lower angle, fills in hard shadows on the other side of the subject's face that the key light has caused. The backlight can be used to light the backdrop and/or the subject's hair and is used to create a sense of depth and some degree of 'separation' from the subject and the background. In more frugal circumstances, using just one light as a key light with a reflector to bounce light back into the shadow side of the face is entirely possible.

The quality of the light can be modified using a range of accessories such as softboxes, umbrellas and beauty dishes, all of which are available in different shapes and sizes. Start simple and build on that.

BASIC STUDIO LIGHTING

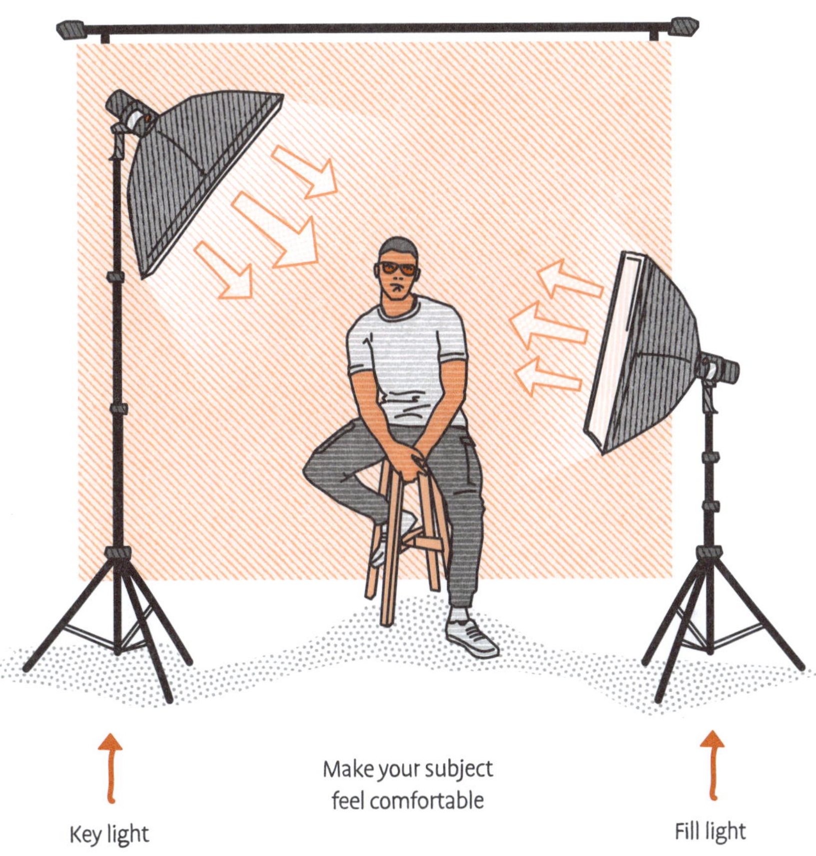

Key light

Make your subject
feel comfortable

Fill light

What makes a good portrait, and how can I make one?

That's a great question and one that's quite hard to answer. While you can use many tips, tricks and techniques to make a portrait technically sound, a good portrait – a picture that reveals an aspect of the sitter's personality – is often down to the human connection the photographer made with the subject.

How do I do that?

It can be difficult and requires skills that aren't necessarily photographic. Asking questions, getting to know your subject and spending time with them will help you better understand their personality and inform what you want to portray. A conversation can also be an excellent way to relax your subject and make them feel comfortable with you. Not everybody likes having their photo taken, and this can make them look uneasy and nervous. Putting time into getting to know them can be invaluable whether you're photographing a stranger or someone you already know.

But I don't always have time to build a 'relationship'.

Sometimes, especially when working on the streets or when travelling, it can be more of a challenge. However, there are ways to quickly build trust, even if you don't speak the same language. A simple nod or hand gesture can be enough to make a connection.

To smile or not to smile?

It depends on the vibe you're trying to evoke and what the purpose of the photo is. Serious, contemplative portraits tend to work better without a big, beaming grin, a quietly confident smile might suit a corporate headshot and an explosive expression of joy from a happy child makes the perfect snapshot. Whatever the vibe, a forced and unnatural smile will always look forced and unnatural.

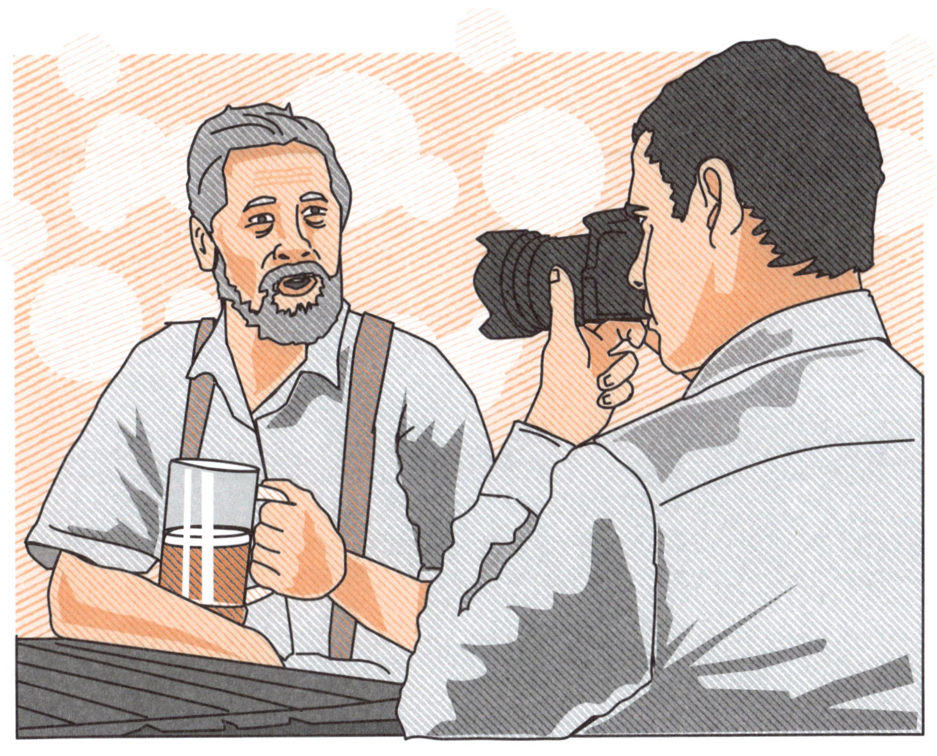

Make your subject feel relaxed by talking and engaging with them

How to photograph: The landscape

How do I start with landscape photography?

It's a big subject and one that's very popular. There are so many ways to approach landscape photography that we could write a book on this subject alone. In the meantime, let's look at the basics to get you started. When people first get into landscape photography, they often aspire to take photos at honeypot locations worldwide, popularized by glossy photo magazines. While this can be a reasonably fun way to hone your skills, it can also be rather one-dimensional. It's better to think of what the land means to you and how you want to connect to it photographically, whether you're drawn to wild and rugged mountainscapes, romantic rural vistas or gritty urban scenes.

What kit do I need?

Let's break this down based on the idea of a classic landscape photograph in the traditional sense. We'll talk about other approaches to landscape photography too, so don't panic if the conventional way isn't your thing.

Camera

Generally, landscape photography is about capturing large amounts of detail and subtle nuances of tone, light and colour, so high-resolution cameras tend to be the go-to.

Lenses

For capturing wide vistas, the 24mm wide-angle is the standard go-to lens for many photographers. However, the compressed, flattening effect of longer telephoto lenses can look great too. Whatever you take, try not to take too much – it'll get heavy if you're out hiking. Consider a zoom lens such as a 24–70mm, which covers both wide and mid-telephoto.

Tripod

Working in low light at dawn and dusk and with small apertures such as f/16 or f/22 (for maximum depth of field) will no doubt mean slow-ish shutter speeds, so stability and the need for a tripod is inevitable. Aside from stability, a tripod will also help if you plan to use techniques such as focus stacking, HDR or long exposures. A tripod will also slow you down and hopefully make you consider your composition and sense of place more mindfully.

Filters

Neutral-density (ND) filters will help you achieve slow shutter speeds if it's bright and you want a long exposure. ND grads are also very popular with landscape photographers, as they help balance the sky and ground exposure. A polarizing filter can help eliminate reflections and glare while intensifying blue skies, contrast and colour saturation.

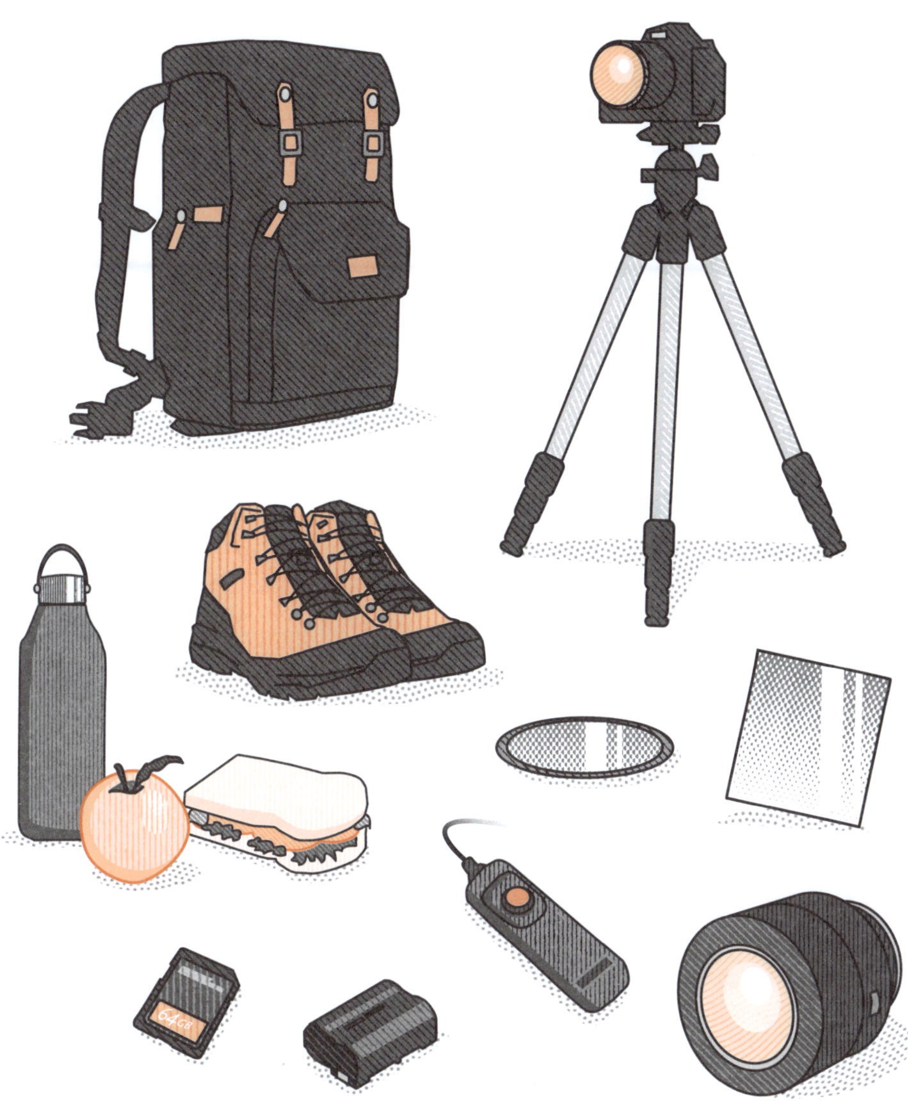

Accessories

Here's a list of essentials: a remote trigger to reduce camera vibration with long exposures; a decent camera backpack, ideally waterproof, with separate compartments for spare clothing, hydration and nourishment; good walking boots and suitable outdoor clothing – nothing hinders the creative flow more than being cold and wet.

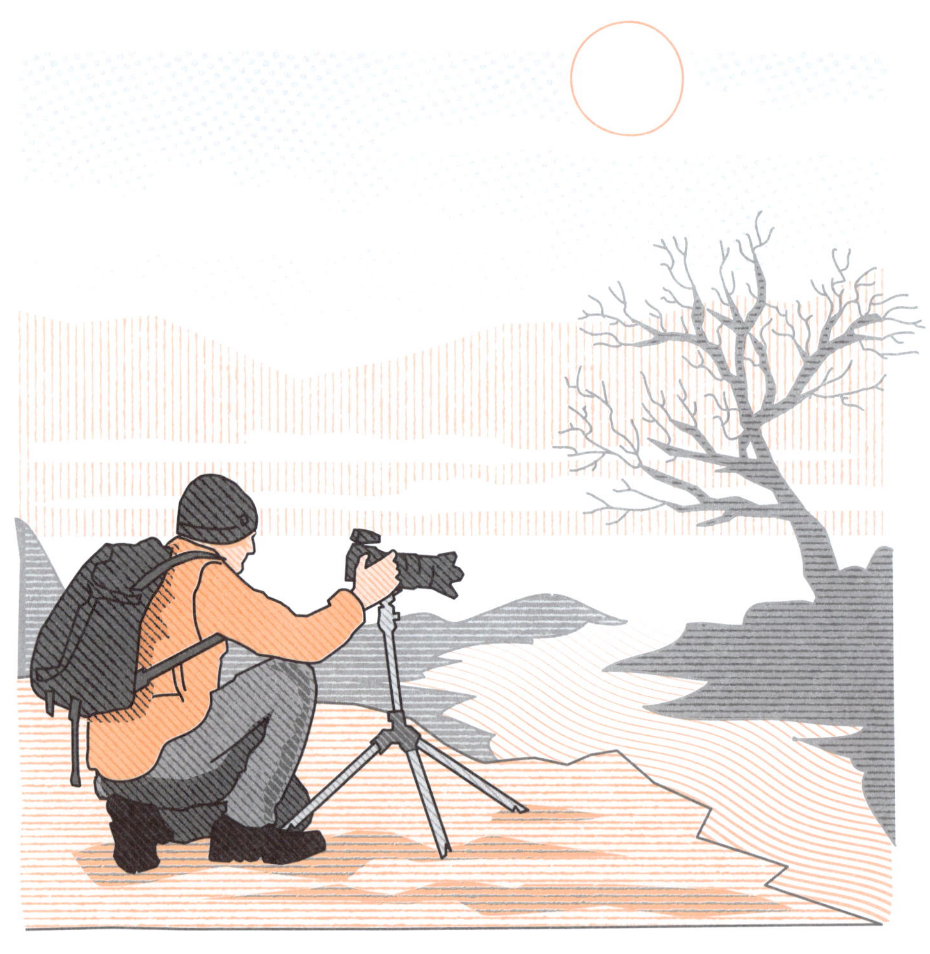

Contemplate your sense of place and try to photograph that feeling

I've got the kit – how do I get started?

First, we'll consider a classic vista and how to approach it in a conventional style. However, I strongly urge you to look beyond the perennial classics and explore the landscape on your own terms.

Research

Start by looking at maps and finding out where to park and how far you'll need to walk and so on, especially if it's a new location for you. While I advocate finding your own vision, looking at how other photographers have interpreted the location can be a good place to start.

Preparation

Pack your camera bag way ahead of the shoot and ensure your batteries are fully charged, memory cards are formatted and you have spares of both.

Time and light

Many landscape photographers like to work at the golden hour (see page 58), when the light is generally more attractive. Several very good smartphone apps, such as PhotoPills, can help you determine when and where the sun will rise and set on specific days. It's very good and worth the modest cost. Inevitably, you'll have to get up early to catch the light!

Position and composition

Once you're at the location, take the time to explore, ideally without your camera. Imagine what the image will look like with your wide-angle lens if you're going for a wide vista. Look for elements in the landscape that you can use as foreground interest – a characterful rock, for example, or other elements that might make good leading lines such as streams or roads. Set up your tripod and start composing.

Making the exposure

It's not just a question of pressing the shutter release – you'll need to think about how you want your image to look too. Is there a difference in brightness between the sky and the ground, and if so, is it enough to warrant using an ND grad filter to balance it out? Do you want to use a polarizer? Do you want a long exposure to blur moving clouds and water? These are creative decisions that you'll need to make. Many of them are subjective, so it's down to you and your creative ambition.

The 'classic' landscape is okay, but how do I explore it on my terms?

So, you've nailed the basics, and you can get a landscape that looks broadly like everybody else's, and you want to dig deeper.

Yep, that's right!

The landscape is a much broader subject than just 'classic' vistas in wild and rugged landscapes. The genre can include everything from parking lots and suburban sprawl to industrial topographies and everything in between. It can be beautiful, ugly, political or poetic.

Take the time to explore the land and get to know it, especially if it's a space new to you, ideally over a long period. Put your camera away and use your other senses to build a sense of place as you encounter it. Use your hearing, smell and touch to build an impression. Then ask yourself how this makes you feel and how you can translate that into a photograph. This process will inform aspects of your creative process, from selecting the subject matter and choosing a point of view and composition to what techniques you might call on from your creative repertoire (or this book!).

Any other tips?

I often call on the wise words of the American photographer and writer Robert Adams. Adams was one of the *New Topographics*, a bunch of photographers working in the 1970s. Their work is interesting and worth looking at. Adams wrote an excellent book called *Beauty in Photography*. In the book, he talks about what makes interesting and engaging landscape photographs. It's good advice and something to ponder when contemplating your landscape work.

Adams suggests that an interesting and engaging landscape photograph should work on three levels: geography, autobiography and metaphor. By geography, he's talking about the topography, the light, the weather, and so on. By autobiography, he's speaking about how you feel about the place where you are and how you respond to it. By metaphor, he's suggesting that the image could present alternative meanings.

He suggests that these criteria can create one-dimensional and potentially boring images independently of one another. However, when all three elements are working together, an image can become interesting. In principle, this is a good, solid approach to keep in the back of your mind when working in the landscape – or anywhere else, for that matter.

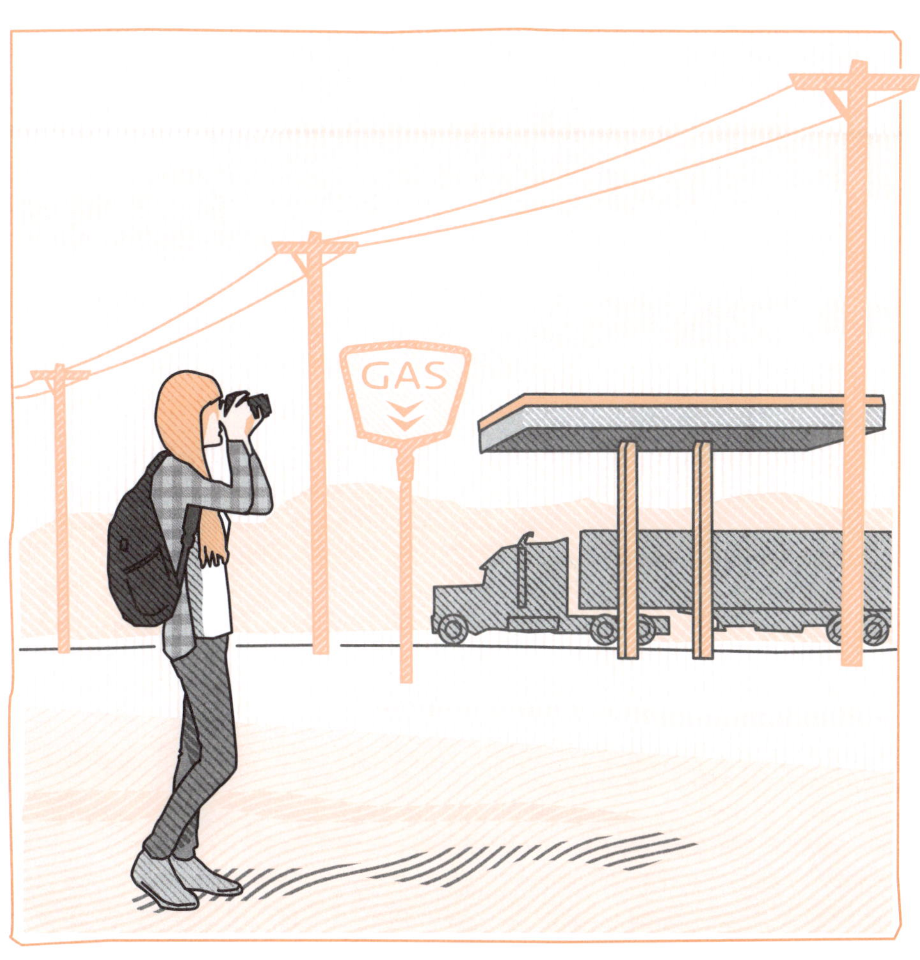

Seemingly humdrum locations can make beautiful photo opportunities

How to photograph: Life on the streets

What is street photography?

I guess you could say photos, typically candid, made on the streets fall into this interesting sub-genre. Some people seem to get strangely hung up on classification, but just go into the streets and take photos – it's that simple and can be great fun, and there is so much to photograph. Open your eyes, learn to look and eventually you'll start 'seeing' images everywhere.

What's the best camera and lens for street photography?

Size and weight are key considerations, along with unobtrusiveness. Leica rangefinder cameras are often touted as the ultimate street cameras, but they're staggeringly expensive, and there are plenty more affordable alternatives. Typically, a slightly wider angle of view, such as 35mm or 28mm, is often used by street photographers. You may have to react super-fast, so get to know your equipment inside out so you don't miss a shot fiddling with settings. Some photographers use zone-focusing techniques (see hyperfocal focusing on page 74) to take photos quickly without the complication of focusing – even super-fast autofocus modes on modern cameras can sometimes be too slow.

Is it okay to photograph people on the streets?

In many countries, photographing someone in a public space without permission is fine and within the law. However, it's worth checking local privacy laws if you're visiting a new country. Regardless of the laws, it's good practice to be respectful and considerate when photographing fellow human beings and representing them truthfully. Treat people like you'd like to be treated yourself. In the tradition of street photography, where happenstance and the chance juxtaposition of a person and their surroundings might create an attractive image, it's a challenge to seek permission or engage with the person first. You'll have to judge this. Some photographers are aggressive in their approach, shoving cameras and flashguns in people's faces. While this may be within the law, it's not very nice.

What's the best way to get started with street photography?

Some photographers like to stake out a location and wait for events to unfold, while others prefer to pound the streets, seeking out opportunities. If you're getting started, try both approaches and see what works for you. Look at the work of some of the great street photographers and see what resonates most with you. Maybe it's people, buildings, cafe scenes, humour or surreal juxtapositions.

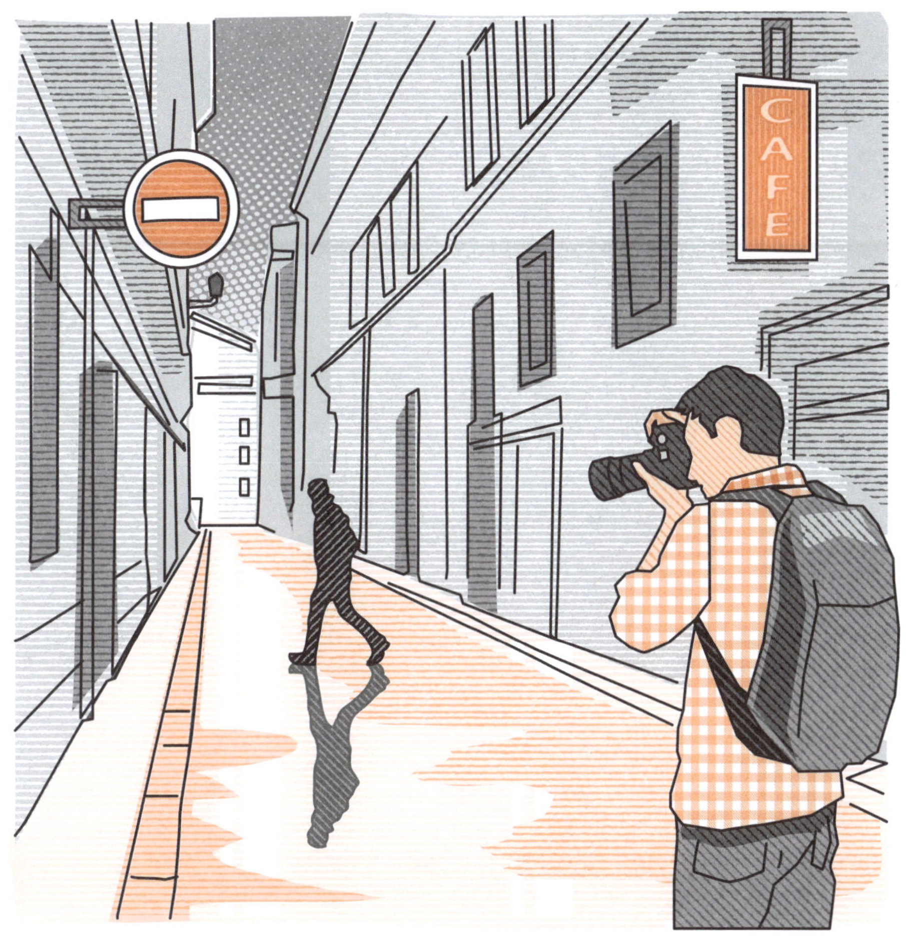

The streets are alive with photographic opportunities

Which photographers do you recommend looking at?

The French photographer and Magnum Photos founder Henri Cartier-Bresson is considered to be the 'godfather' of street photography. Check out his work, but also look at that of Bruce Gilden, Joel Meyerowitz, Helen Levitt, Vivian Maier and Saul Leiter to whet your appetite and get some ideas and inspiration.

How to photograph: Food

What's the best way to shoot food?
This is another big subject with lots of creative potential to explore. You could photograph a chef at work in their kitchen, a street vendor selling hot dogs, the hustle and bustle of a fresh fruit-and-veg market or a plate of the finest food exquisitely prepared for your pleasure. Open any cookbook, and you'll see pages of mouth-watering photographs created to whet your appetite.

So how do I make mouth-watering images?
First, look at the food and explore it. It's much like making a portrait or even a landscape photograph in that you want to seek out its essence. Ask yourself what the 'hero' of the dish is? Use the hero as the foundation and build the image from that focal point. The setting and props should complement but not distract from the subject – for example, a rustic farmhouse pot roast will need a different approach than a Michelin-starred minimalist delight. Think about context, colour, light and composition.

What about composition and point of view?
There are many ways to approach composition (see page 62), and all the skills you've learned in this book will come into play. Depth of field can be a useful tool in your creative armoury, especially if you choose a low angle. A wide aperture such as f/2.8 will create a shallow depth of field, separating the subject from the background and diffusing potentially distracting elements. However, just because the background is blurred doesn't mean it's not important – it's a vital part of the image and helps create context. Look at the blurred parts of the image and pay attention to them too. Think about colour and colour harmony.

An odd number of objects can be easier to compose than an even number. Take three objects and see how much easier it is to arrange them into a satisfying arrangement than with four.

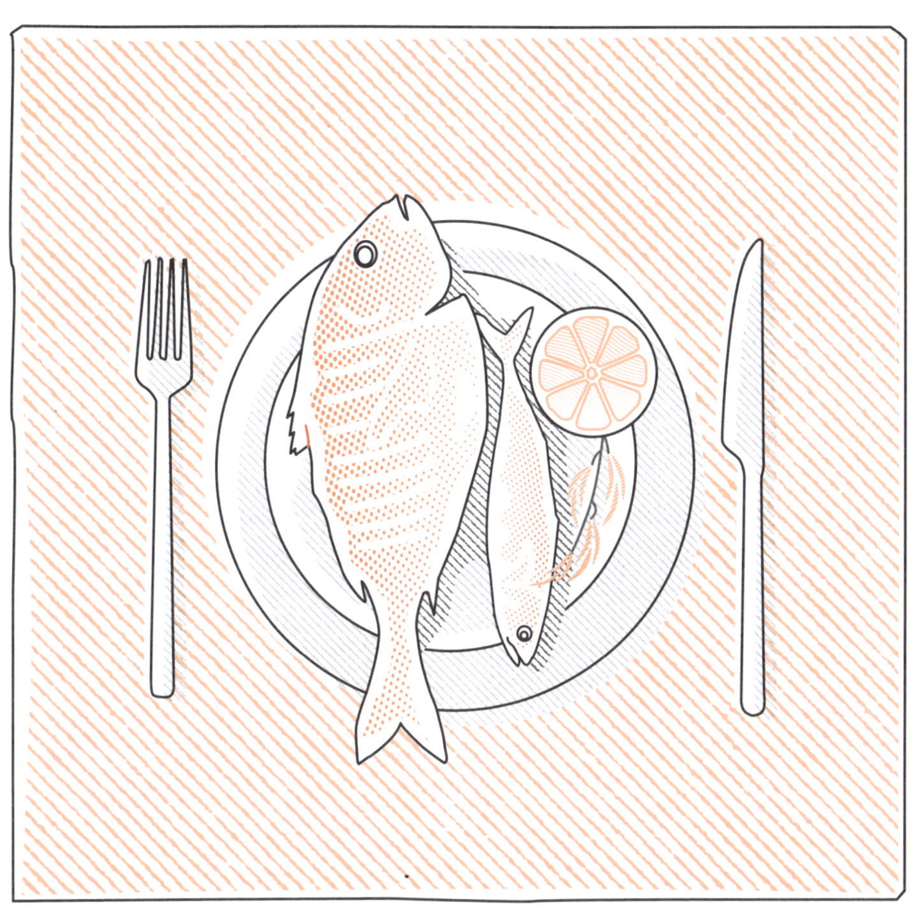

Practise your food photography at home

Do I need a bunch of fancy equipment and lighting?

Absolutely not! Some professional food photographers will use fancy studios and complex lighting set-ups, but it's not necessary. Natural light is a better option in the first instance, so master this before you think about using studio lights. A north-facing window is ideal, as the light will be slightly flatter and more diffused. You may want to use some modifiers, such as reflectors, to 'bounce' light onto the subject and fill in shadow areas. You can easily make a reflector using tin foil or a piece of white card.

How to photograph: Close-ups

Exploring the miniature world in detail can reveal a wealth of photo opportunities.

What do I need to photograph close-up?
Inevitably, you will need a macro lens to take close-up photos. A macro lens allows you to focus really close to the subject, so its minimum focus distance is much closer than a regular lens. You may have heard people talk about a 1:1 macro. This effectively means that the magnification ratio of the subject will be recorded at the same size on the camera's sensor.

Which macro lens should I get?
True macro lenses are prime lenses and are available in different focal lengths – your choice depends on budget and what you want to photograph. If, for example, you have the ambition to photograph butterflies in the wild, you may find a telephoto macro lens such as a 110mm better, as you can position yourself further away from the subject without spooking it. But if you're photographing inanimate objects in a small home studio, you may want to be closer to the subject and plump for a wider-angle macro such as a 60mm.

Is there an alternative if I can't afford a macro lens?
Using a reversal ring is a cheaper alternative. It's essentially an adaptor ring that allows you to mount your lens the other way around on your camera. It'll look a bit odd and has some limitations, but this will effectively turn your standard lens into a macro lens. You could also consider a close-up filter, which is also relatively inexpensive. They're a bit like attaching reading glasses to the front of your lens. Both are good, cheap ways to get started with macro, but if it fires you up and you love this kind of photography, consider saving for a proper macro lens.

What about an extension tube?
Extension tubes are another relatively cost-effective way to turn a regular lens into a macro lens. An extension tube won't affect the image quality. However, it will reduce the amount of light entering the camera, so you'll need to factor this into your workflow and exposure calculations.

GET CLOSE UP WITH A MACRO LENS

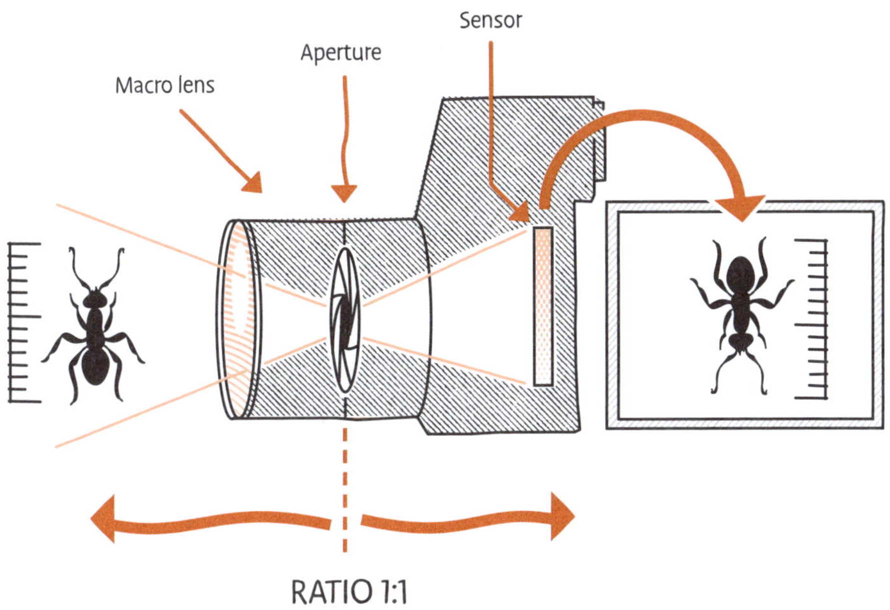

I've heard of focus stacking – what's that?

It's a great technique that can be used to make super-sharp macro shots. Typically, when you use a macro lens in an extreme close-up situation, the depth of field will be very narrow, even at small apertures such as f/16. The idea behind focus stacking is to take multiple shots at different points of focus and then 'stack' them using specialist software. The software will cleverly select the sharp parts of each image and create a composition that appears super-sharp from front to back. It's a bit fiddly and takes some practice to get right. However, most modern digital cameras will feature a function that automates the process. All you have to do is specify a starting focus point and the number of shots you want to take from that point and the camera will change the focus, often a microscopic amount between each shot. After importing the individual images into software such as Adobe Photoshop or Helicon Focus, it will blend them together.

Look at the amazing work of Levon Biss for inspiration – some of his images are made up of thousands of individual photos. They are mind-boggling.

What's a ring flash?

It's a specialist flash often used by forensic and medical photographers who frequently use close-up photography. As the name suggests, the flash bulb is ring-shaped and designed to fit around a lens rather than on top of a camera. In most extreme close-up situations, a hotshoe-mounted flash wouldn't illuminate the subject, as the light would effectively miss the subject. A flash around the lens allows a close-up photographer to get much closer. Not only will the light hit the subject, it will also be evenly distributed. Interestingly, some fashion and portrait photographers have adopted ring flash too. Its harsh and slightly crude aesthetic, circular catchlights in the subject's eyes and the halo-like shadow it casts have a certain allure.

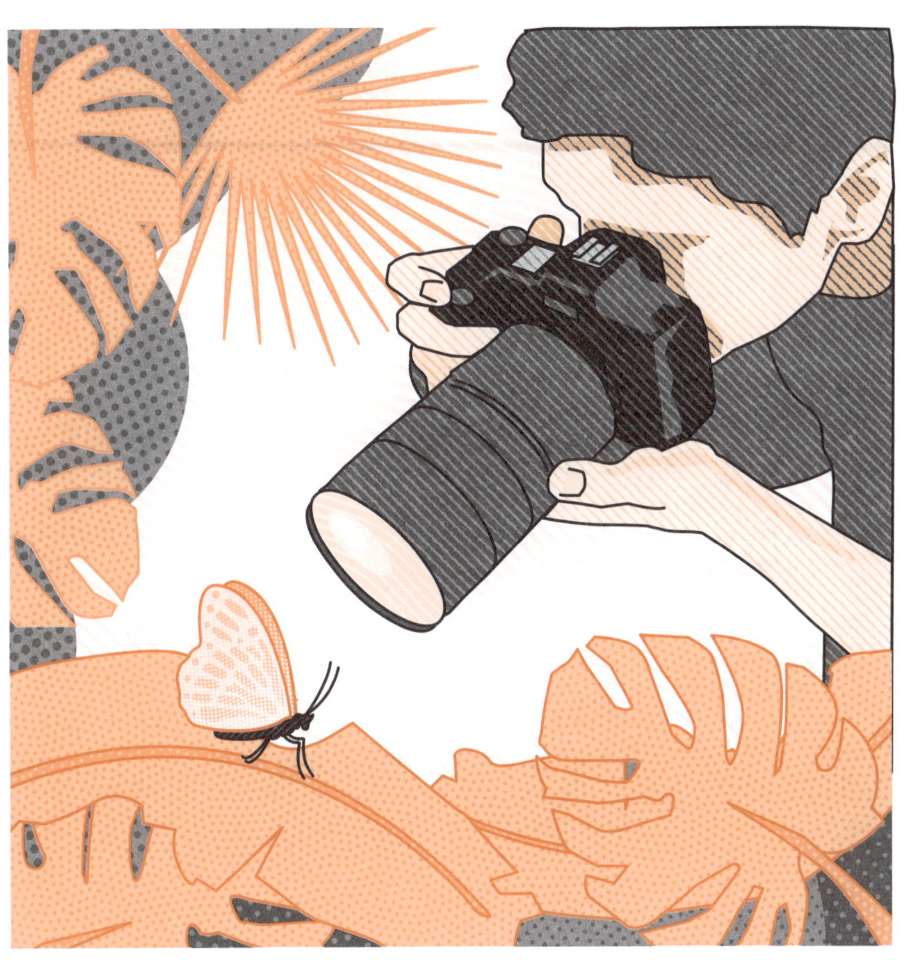

Exploring the close-up world with a macro lens can be awe-inspiring

How to photograph: Wildlife

How do I get into wildlife photography?
The best place to start is close to home. Hone your skills with the wildlife in your garden or local park. The idea of 'wildlife photography' often conjures exotic images of lions in Africa, polar bears in the Arctic and penguins in Antarctica. However, there is a plethora of wildlife wonders closer to home.

What kit do I need?
A long telephoto lens is the most helpful specialist kit to contemplate purchasing. Animals in a natural environment, even your back garden, will spook easily, so being able to shoot from a distance will help you enormously. You'll also often see wildlife photographers staked out in camouflage hides. These hides can help disguise your presence. Big lenses are heavy to hold, especially if you're waiting for a shot for a long time, so a tripod or monopod helps too.

Big telephoto lenses can be costly, so if you're just dipping your toes in the water with wildlife photography, you may want to think about renting one for a weekend in the first instance.

You'll also need to understand your camera so it's second nature. It's often the case that after hours of patiently waiting for the moment, the 'action' is over swiftly. You'll need to be on the ball or run the risk of missing the shot entirely as you fumble for focus or get lost in menus.

Many cameras have a bunch of features that can help. Functions such as focus tracking and continuous shooting will help. Focus tracking does just that and can be useful for following an animal and keeping it in focus. However, despite its usefulness, it still needs practice, and nothing replaces the inherent knowledge of being able to anticipate where the animal will move. Continuous shooting mode will take photos continuously while your finger presses the shutter. This can be a dozen or so frames per second. If you're shooting large raw files, this will use up a lot of memory, and the images will start to buffer as they wait to load onto your memory card. This is also why it's helpful to use high-speed memory cards.

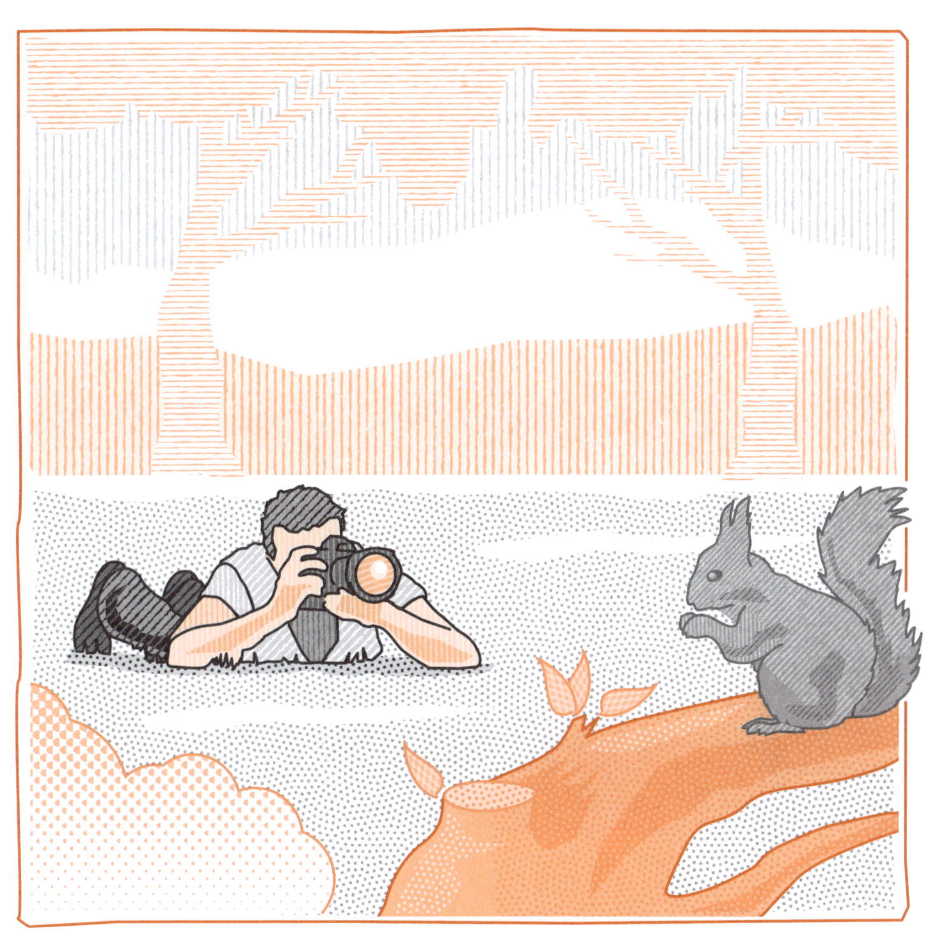

Hone your skills on local wildlife in your garden or nearby park

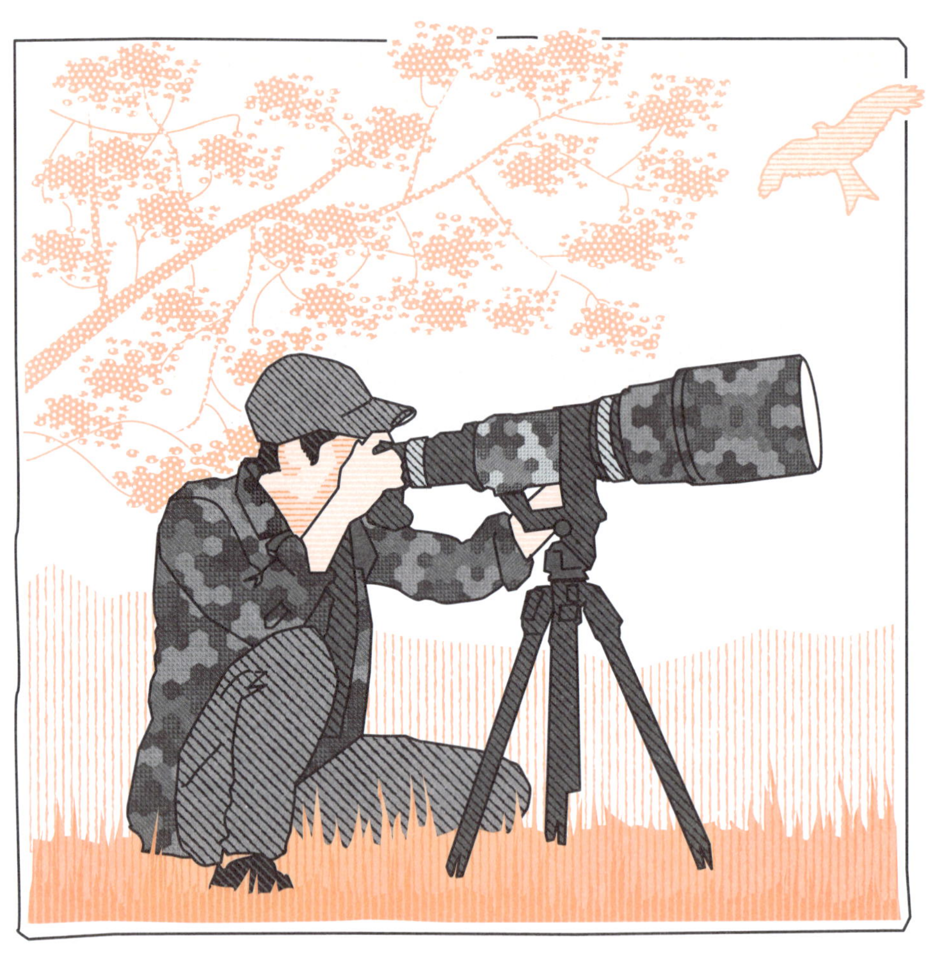

A long telephoto (such as 200–600mm) is vital for some subjects

I've got the kit – now what?

Understanding the behaviour of the animal you're photographing is vital to capturing decent wildlife images. Many wildlife photographers have a solid background in zoology and have extensive knowledge to inform them. Of course, you don't need to run off and do a degree in zoology, but some research into your intended subject is essential. There's little point in staking it out at midday to photograph a nocturnal animal.

Patience is vital

More than any other type of photography, working with wildlife requires time and patience. Lots of patience. Understanding the behaviour and habits of your subject is helpful. However, there is still no substitute for sticking it out and waiting. Some professional wildlife photographers can spend months in pursuit of the sight of an elusive animal and still have no guarantee of bagging the shot.

Focus on the eyes

Focusing on your subject's eyes will make for a more engaging image. It can be tricky, especially if you're photographing a fast-flying bird. Other skills you will have learned in this book, such as composition and depth of field, will be useful too.

Be kind and ethical

Always respect the animals and their environment and consider their well-being above anything else. Sadly, you may come across workshops where an animal's safety is compromised. For example, some kingfisher photography workshops and tours have been known to lure the bird into diving by placing glass tanks filled with bait just beneath the water's surface. This is dangerous and frankly terrible. Don't encourage it.

Practice

In addition to bundles of patience, you'll also need to practise and then practise some more. Practice is mentioned a lot in this book, but it is with good reason. While there are lots of features on cameras that'll help you, they are no substitute for good, honest practice.

How to photograph: Action

What do I need to know?
Capturing action is a highly skilled art and can be tricky to master. However, some tips, tricks and camera settings can help you.

What are they?
Understanding the sport that you're photographing is incredibly helpful. If you can anticipate and predict where the 'action' is about to happen, you're ahead of the game already. You can prefocus on that area and be ready to bag the shot.

What about the settings on my camera?
The obvious starting point is a fast shutter speed to freeze the action. Naturally, it depends on the sport you're photographing, but start at about 1/500sec and experiment from there. You'll need to adjust your aperture and ISO accordingly or switch to shutter-priority mode and let the camera figure it out for you.

What about drive modes?
Action is what drive modes are made for. Switch to continuous or burst mode and keep your finger pressed on the shutter button as the action happens. Hey presto, you've nailed it. Well, it's not that simple, and there are other things to consider too. Different cameras will shoot different amounts of frames per second (fps), and some cameras can shoot up to about 13fps, which is pretty impressive. However, if you're shooting large files, your memory will card will fill up quickly along with your camera's buffer, and this can slow you down and potentially mean missing the shot. Much of this depends on your camera's processing speed, its buffer size and the write speed of your memory card. Experiment and see what the parameters are for your kit.

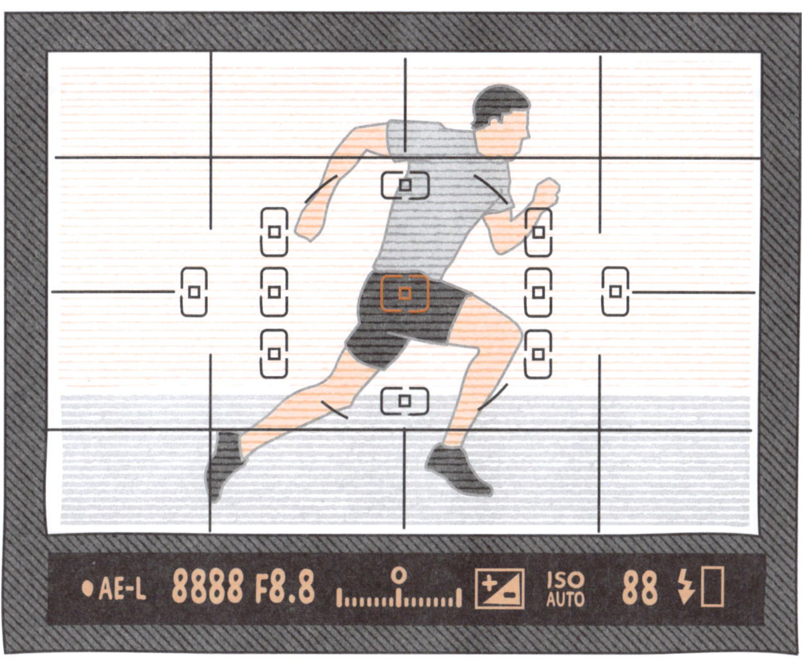

Focus tracking is useful for action shots

What about focus?
Focusing on a fast-moving subject is tricky, but there are some tools to help. Switch the autofocus to continuous mode to track moving objects. This can be a game-changer, but how sophisticated and helpful it is varies from camera to camera.

Anything else?
Yes, regardless of all the bells and whistles listed here, there is no substitute for practising, especially with action and sports photography. These features are there to help you, not do it for you. You do have to put in the leg work and hone your skills.

What's 'panning'?
Panning is an excellent technique used by action photographers. The idea is that you move your camera in the direction of the action while focusing and tracking the subject, resulting in a sharp subject and motion-blurred background. The movement of the camera should, in theory, blur the background and, with skillful tracking of the subject, keep the subject sharp. This can give a dynamic sense of movement and energy. However, it does require some skill to get right. In the first instance, practise on a relatively easy subject – a willing friend on a bicycle would be perfect. Have them ride past you, and as they do so, follow their movement.

What shutter speed should I use to pan?
The answer depends on how fast your subject is moving and how far away it is from the camera. Practice is, without a doubt, the best solution. In this instance, you'll be better off switching your camera to its shutter-priority mode (see page 46).

Are there any features on a camera to help?
Yes, most modern digital cameras will have some sort of focus tracking, and this can be incredibly helpful. Also, switch to continuous shooting mode so that when you press the shutter, your camera will fire continuously, sometimes upwards of ten frames per second, depending on your camera.

Anything else I should be aware of?
Try to keep your feet in one spot and rotate from your waist as you follow the subject. Keep your camera's motion smooth so it flows in the direction of the subject and try to follow the subject before and after the point you want to capture, firing the shutter continuously. It's not easy, but the results can be worth it.

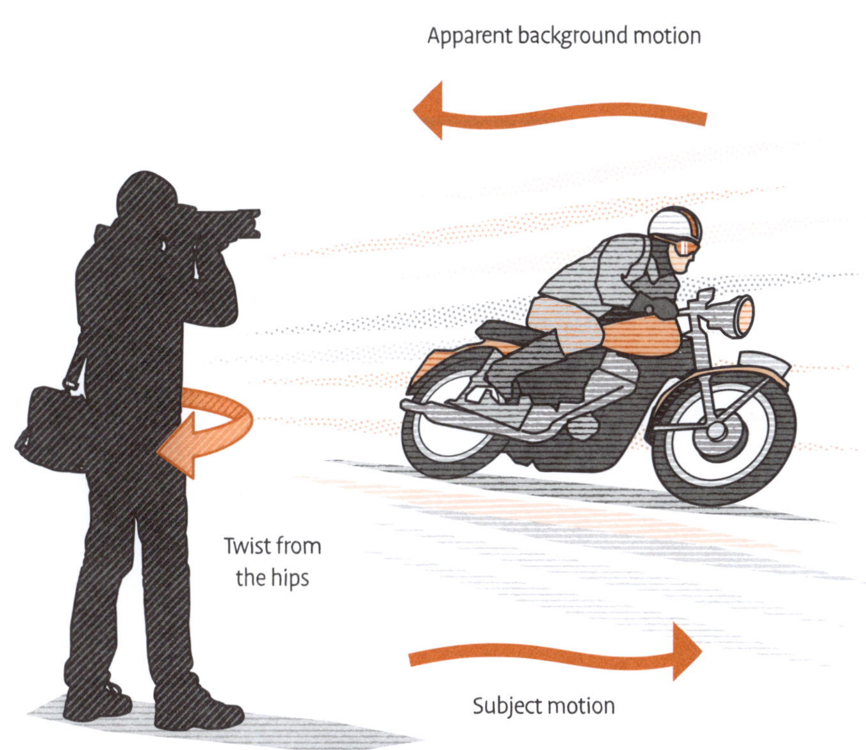

Use motion bur to add a dynamic twist

How to photograph: Travel

What's the best way to think about travel photography?
Think about the journey as much, if not more so, than the destination. The journey is often more interesting photographically. Also, don't get hung up on the idea that you must travel to exotic locations. Even a daily commute or walk to the shops is 'travel' – use these experiences to hone your skills.

Open your eyes...
One of the great things about travelling and photographing in places you've never been to is that you tend to see and notice things that you probably wouldn't do on your home turf. Travelling seems to have this effect on many people. Enjoy it. Embrace it.

The spirit of place
While the postcard racks and tourist brochures can be a good starting point in knowing what to photograph, they are only a springboard. Look beyond the regular tourist haunts, get off the beaten track and explore. Talk to people, take their photographs, listen to their stories and try to incorporate that into a portrait. Buildings, food, people, street scenes and even more mundane subjects such as bus shelters, shop windows and gas stations are all part of the travel experience. Photograph them too and use them to help tell the story.

If you meet people and take their portraits, give them some way to contact you so you can send them a copy of the picture when you get home. A simple business card is inexpensive to produce and can lead to lively long-distance friendships.

Be a ruthless picture editor!
Imagine that a picture editor at a big glossy magazine has to put an eight-page feature together on a destination. How many images do you think they might show? Probably no more than 20. This is how you should think too. Nobody wants to see 500+ holiday snaps, but 20 or so artfully selected images can tell a concise and eloquent story. Think about the types of images you include; think of pace and rhythm. Wide establishing shots can set the scene while small details, characterful portraits and other such images can give your story nuance and richness.

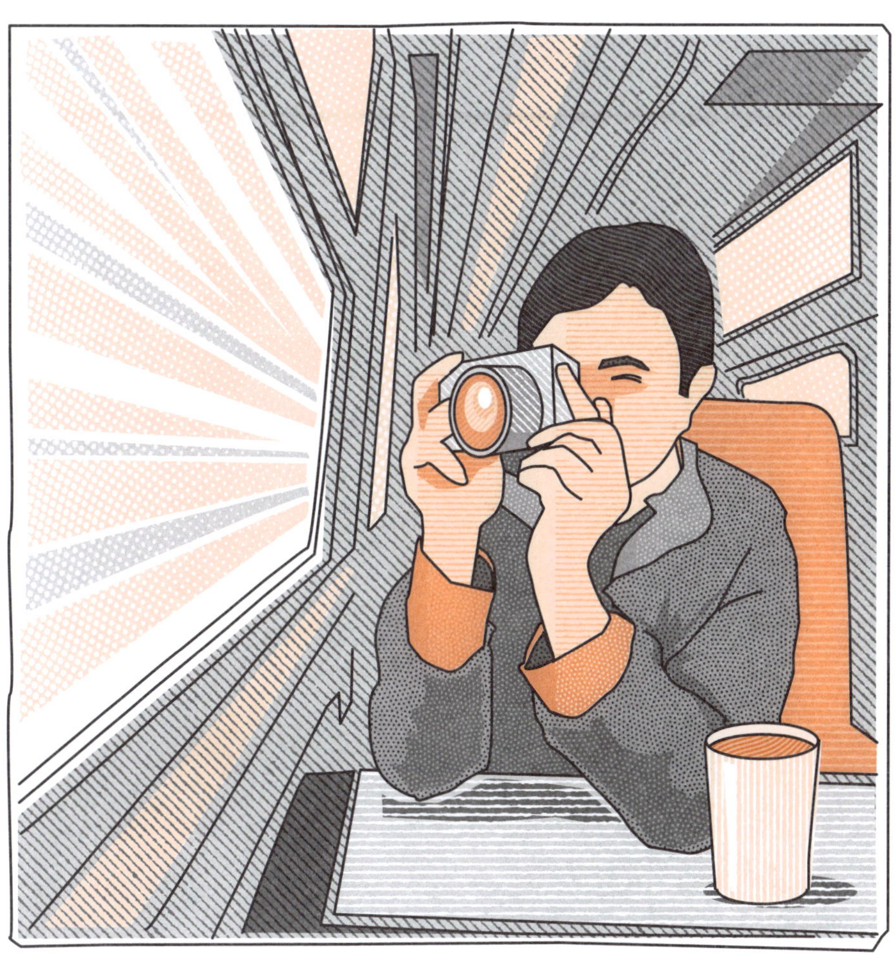

Consider the journey, not just the destination

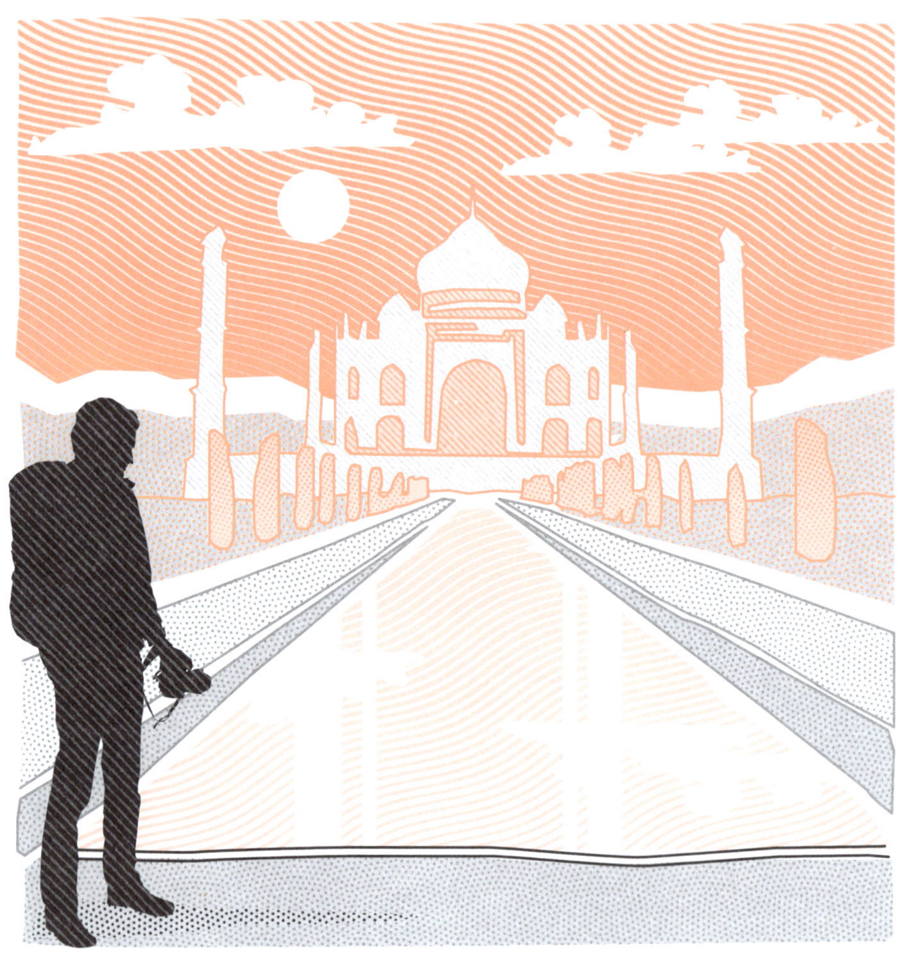

Try to find your own way of ‘seeing’ iconic locations

What about the practical aspects of travel photography?

Whether pounding the streets on a city break in a fabulous European city, hiking in the Himalayas or grooving on the Trans-Siberian Railway, you want to keep your kit simple and lightweight. You do not need to lug all your lenses around with you. Try using just one lens. For example, a 35mm is a handy all-purpose focal length for 'travel' photography. Sure, there may be moments when you might wish you had the extra reach of a telephoto, but you'll soon learn to work within the limitations and simply find a way to move closer or further away with your feet. Aside from being a lot easier to carry around all day, the discipline of using one lens will make you a better photographer.

Should I get special camera insurance for travel photography?

It's worth checking whether your household insurance covers your kit. If not, there are plenty of options for bespoke camera insurance, and it's worth the peace of mind. Equipment is replaceable, so if you do find yourself in an awkward position, don't fight back. It's another good reason not to carry too much kit around. Some photographers will make their kit look old, battered and less attractive to thieves using electrical tape to cover up recognizable brand logos and so on. On this point, always be aware of your surroundings – it's easy to wander off on a line of visual enquiry into a street or district that may be less safe.

What should I wear?

Good shoes are vital. A day's shooting in a new city can easily involve 6 miles (10km) or more of walking. Clothing should be relevant to the location and weather.

How to photograph: Still life

What exactly is still life photography?
It's a sub-genre of photography that essentially involves photographing inanimate objects. Before the invention of photography, artists gravitated to the subject, and it has a long history in the art world. With photography, it can be a lot of fun and a great way to flex your creative muscles, hone your skills and express yourself.

How do I get started, and what do I need?
Like so many aspects of creative photography, there are many ways to get started. In the first instance, consider whether you want to seek out still life subjects that already exist in the world or if you prefer creating set-ups in a home studio.

If you're interested in the concept of 'found' still life, keep your eyes open for potential subjects as you walk around with your camera. For example, the condiments on a cafe table in the right light can be sublimely beautiful and evocative, or the happenstance arrangement of random objects in a junk shop window might pique your interest. Approaching still life this way is all about looking, seeing and being open and responsive to recognize and acknowledge a potential shot when you come across it. On the flip side, working in a controlled studio environment is another way to work with still life. Creating a makeshift still life studio at home is relatively easy.

What do I need to make a home studio for shooting still life?
Start with the objects you want to photograph. Consider the background, lighting, arrangement of the objects and the composition. Working in a controlled environment has many advantages, and you can contemplate, experiment and try things in a way that you simply cannot with other forms of photography. It can be useful to start with a sketch. Keep it simple and start with a few objects, a plain background and one light. A desk lamp is fine to get started. You can also introduce modifiers to reflect, bounce and 'mould' the light. You can make these easily enough out of pieces of card and tin foil. If you have a tripod, use it. It's easier to arrange and tweak the position of the objects if your camera is static. It will also mean you don't need to worry about slow shutter speeds.

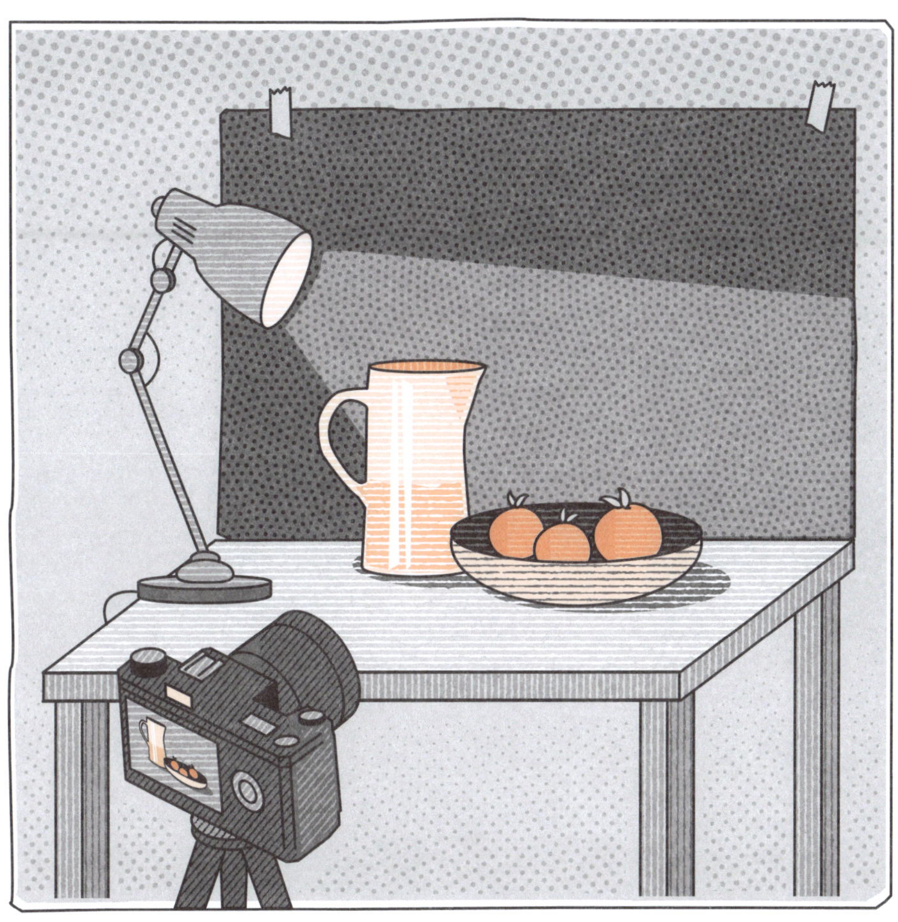

You don't need more than a kitchen table and a desk lamp to get started

Anything else I need?
Getting objects to stay in position can sometimes be a challenge, so some Blu Tack and gaffer tape and/or electrical tape will be your best friends. A dab of Blu Tack underneath a persistently rolling apple or some gaffer tape holding the stem of a flower in place can be lifesavers. Just ensure you can't see it through your camera's viewfinder.

It's not a bad idea to build a store of helpful still life props such as coloured cards, rolls of paper, glass jars, various fabrics, etc. Material can also be useful. Look at how light falls on certain fabrics – velvet looks very different from silk, and both can be used in different situations. Black velvet is brilliant and absorbs light well. Scouring thrift shops is a great way to build a library of props.

How to photograph:
Plants and flowers

What makes a good plant or flower photograph?

Think of plants and flowers as characters and approach them as if you're making a conventional portrait. Consider their personality and ask yourself how you can interpret that photographically.

Should I work on location or in a studio?

Using cut flowers in a studio can be great fun, and implementing some of the skills you'll have honed with still life photography (see page 154), you'll be able to use lights and modifiers to control the light to your creative desire. If you plan on doing a lot of flower photography in a studio-type set-up, think about getting some clamps like those found in science labs – they can help keep things in place – along with tape and coloured card. However, photographing plants and flowers in their environment is also advantageous and feels more natural. Some photographers even take a background into the field, although it's arguably better to include the environment. Also, don't be shy to be even more expansive and include a wide vista of a garden in your repertoire.

When working outside, even the slightest wind can be incredibly annoying while focusing on a delicate flower dancing in the breeze.

What's the best lighting for flowers?

It depends on your creative vision and what you want to portray. Some plants, such as spiky cactus, might benefit from a harsh, contrasty light to express their character. However, a soft, diffused light is often best to tease out a delicate flower's beauty. If you're in a studio, there are many ways to control light using modifiers and diffusers. It's more of a challenge in the wild but still possible. Ideally, a dull, cloud-covered day will act as the best diffuser. If it's sunny, you can improvise with a pop-up diffuser or a reflector to fill in shadow areas.

Depth of field

Generally, you'll work quite close to your subject so a macro lens might be needed (see page 28). Think about using a wide aperture such as f/2.8 to create a shallow depth of field and blur the background, but as always, keep a keen eye on the background. Even if it's blurred, there will still be dark and light tones or patches of colour from other flowers that will impact the composition.

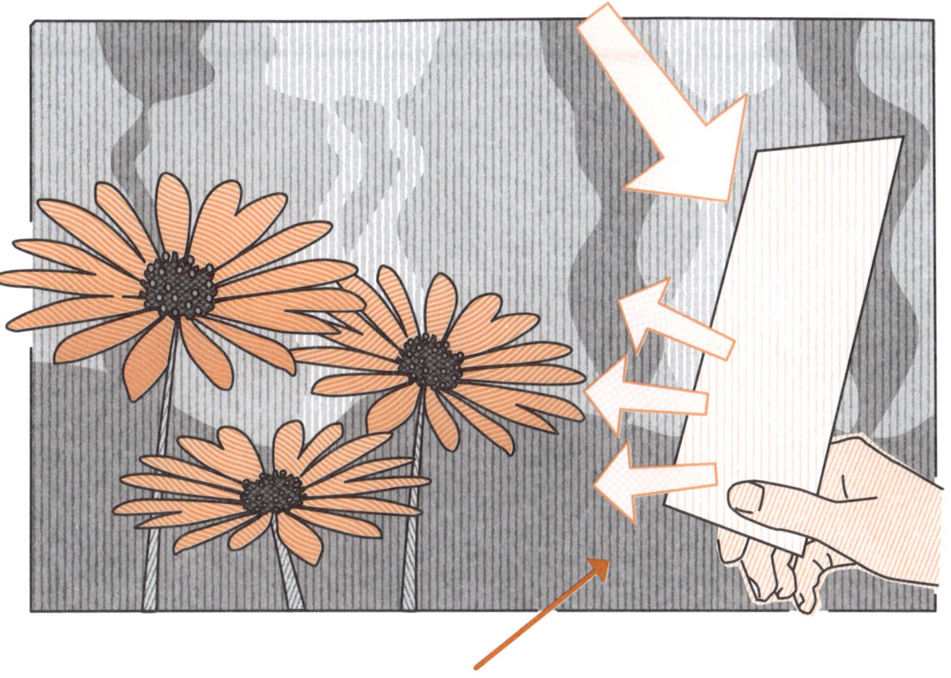

Use a sheet of white card as an improvised reflector
to bounce light onto your subject

How to photograph:
In low light

How much light is needed?
If you want to handhold your camera without introducing unwanted camera shake, use your lens's focal length as a way of guesstimating the slowest shutter speed you'll be able to use. For example, if you're using an 85mm lens, don't shoot at anything slower than 1/80sec. Cameras and lenses today feature image stabilization, which will help, but it's still worth working out the slowest shutter speed you'll be able to handhold without any camera shake.

Is that why a wide-aperture lens is useful?
Spot on! And that's why lenses with wider apertures are called 'fast' lenses, as you'll be able to use faster shutter speeds. Of course, this will compromise your depth of field (see page 50), but it's a good reason to purchase a lens with a wide aperture such as f/2.8 or f/1.4. Annoyingly, 'faster' lenses are more expensive too.

What if I don't have a 'fast' lens or want to use a wide aperture?
There are several options: use a tripod, introduce lights or increase your ISO.

Can you explain the pros and cons of these options and which one I should use?
As always, it depends on your creative vision and circumstances. A tripod is a great tool (see page 32). Simply mount your camera on a tripod to keep it steady, and you'll be able to use shutter speeds that are so slow you'll be able to have a quick nap while you're taking a photo. However, you may not have a tripod or want to carry it around, or your subject might not be something that will stay still for seconds or even minutes.

Is ISO the answer?
If you don't want to use a tripod, yes. Just crank it up. Cameras are so good at high ISOs these days that you can go quite high before noticing any real image deterioration. Test your camera and find out what your highest acceptable ISO is.

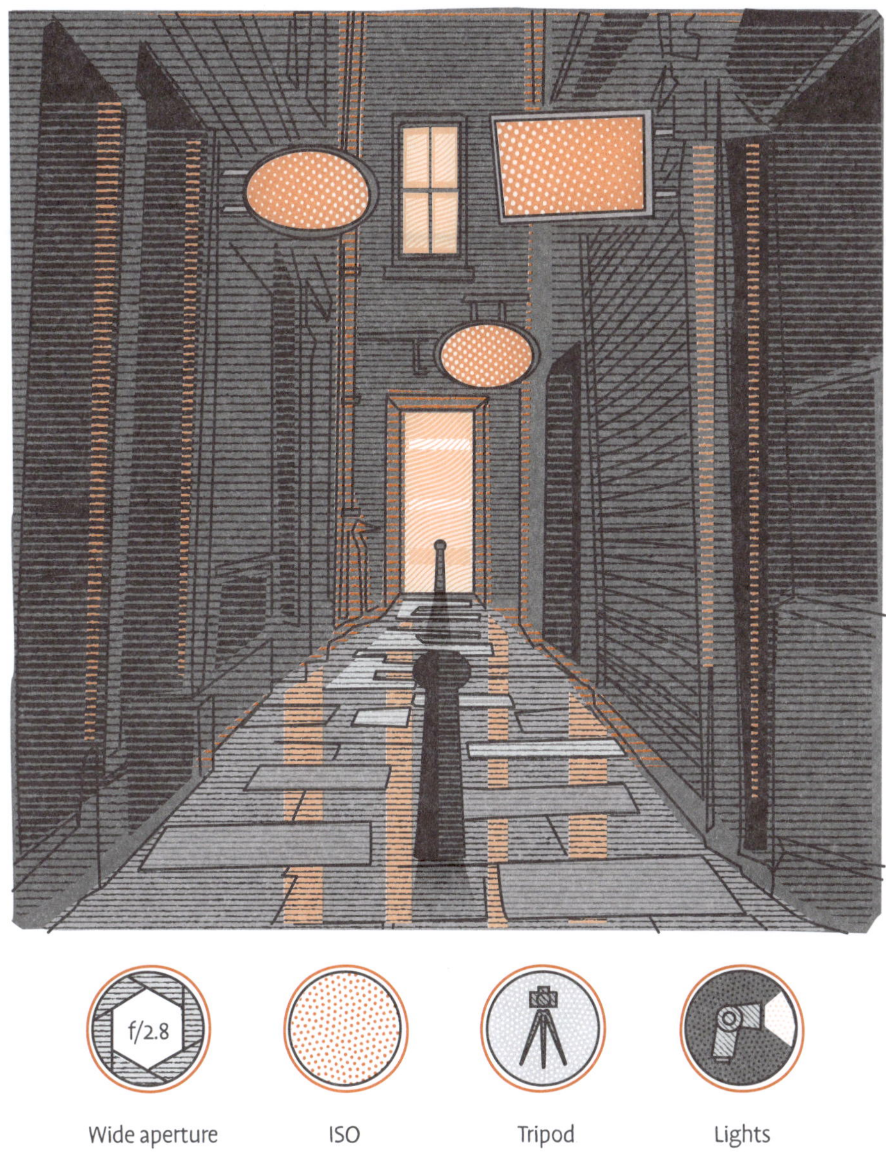

When there's not enough light, you'll have to decide which path to take

How to photograph: Recap

There are so many ways to use photography, whether you want to photograph buildings , landscape, people, action or whatever takes your fancy. The genres highlighted in this section will give you a taste of what to expect. They are a guide to help you get started, they'll point you in the right direction and set you on your path; however, there's much more to discover than can be summarized here, so start your journey with an open and inquisitive mind.

Five top tips

1 If you're new to photography, try all the types in this chapter and get a sense of what you enjoy.

2 Some of the techniques in this section require some fancy kit or accessories, but don't let that put you off. In the first instance, consider renting equipment for a day or two or experimenting with cheaper alternatives.

3 Many photographers offer workshops in their specialist field. Do some research, and if you see a workshop by someone whose work you admire think about attending. It might be the best things you've ever done - other than buy this book, of course!

4 Look at the work of other photographers; see how they make images, and take the time to really analyze their photographs. There's no harm in trying to emulate their work while you find your creative feet. Your own 'voice' and vision will emerge in time.

5 Experiment! The genres discussed in this section and guidelines in it are there to help you get started. The real creativity starts when you challenge the conventions and try something different. It won't always work, but every once in a while, it will, and that's ace.

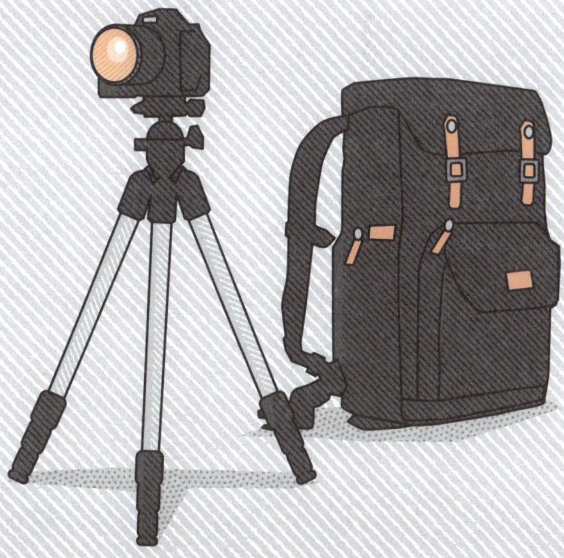

5

POST-PRODUCTION AND MINDFULNESS

The digital darkroom

Most of this book is dedicated to the skills needed to make a photograph at the point of capture. We've looked at the tools and how they work, from cameras and lenses to studio lights, tripods and everything in between. We've explored the intricacies of exposure, the nuances of colour and how to control the look and feel of your photos. We've experimented with some creative ideas and discovered how these skills can be used in a range of disciplines, from sports and wildlife photography to making portraits or being a minimalist. However, the story doesn't end there. There's a whole treasure trove of delights when editing your images, and the digital darkroom adds new and wonderful layers of potential creativity and expression to your work. There are whole books dedicated to this subject alone, but in the few pages left, we'll look at some things to be aware of.

The great American landscape photographer Ansel Adams (1902–84) famously said, 'The negative is the score, and the print is the performance'. He said this long before digital photography was invented, but the principle remains unchanged. Think of your digital camera's raw file as the 'negative and score' in Adams' quote and what you do with it in the digital darkroom as the 'print and performance'. What you do with it can have a massive impact on how your audience views and reads an image. Using image-editing software, it's relatively easy to take a raw file and turn it from a relatively 'straight' image into something monochromatic, moody and gritty, or into something vibrant, light and poetic.

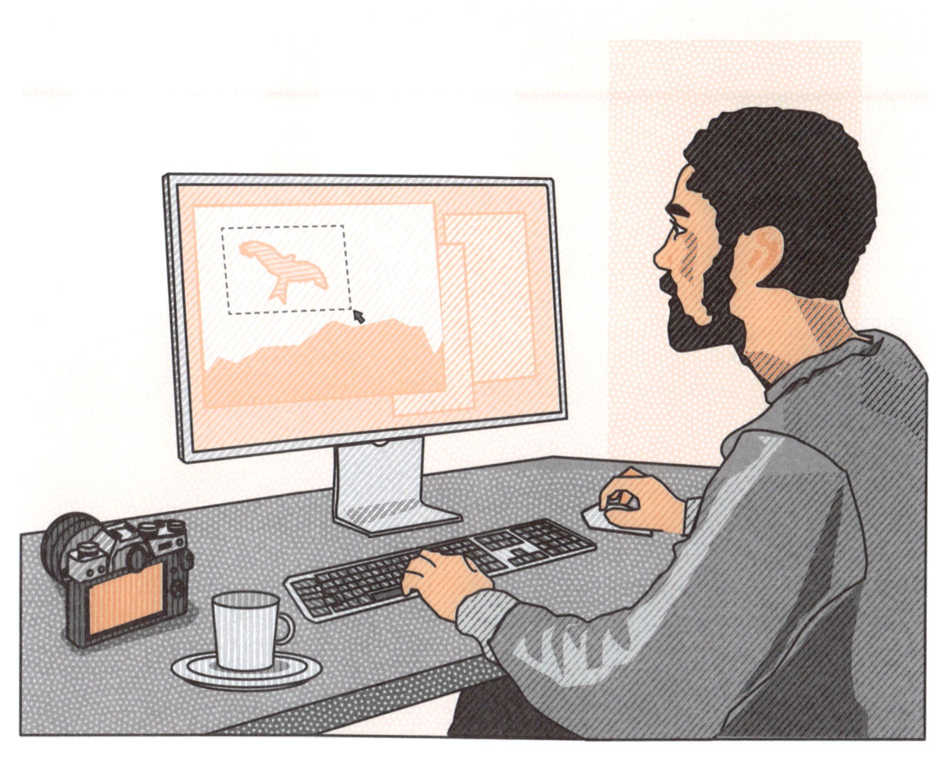

Working in the digital darkroom is also part of the creative process

Image-editing workflow

What kit do I need?
You've spent a fortune on your cameras and lenses, and now you've got to spend money on your digital darkroom. As with the camera kit, you can work to a budget or spend a lot of money. Let's look at the essentials.

Computer
At the very least, you will need a computer and monitor. Processing large raw files is quite intensive work for a computer, so processing power and working memory are crucial considerations.

Should I get a desktop or laptop computer?
It depends. The big advantage of a laptop is that you can work on the move, which for many photographers is beyond useful. However, a desktop with a separate specialist photo monitor will give you more processing power and memory for your money and a nice big screen to work on. There's no right or wrong decision, and whichever route you choose will cost you. Sorry.

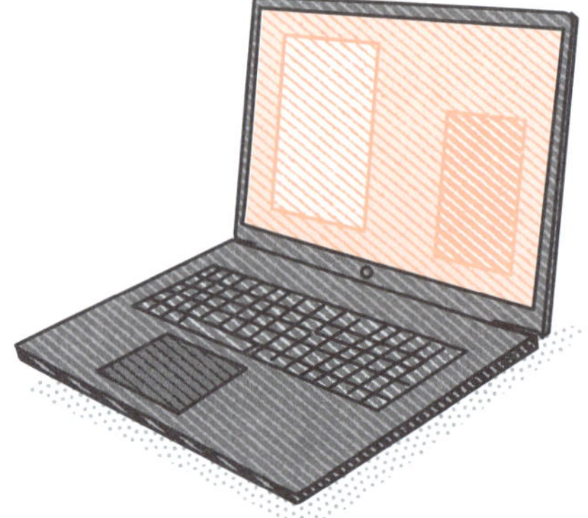

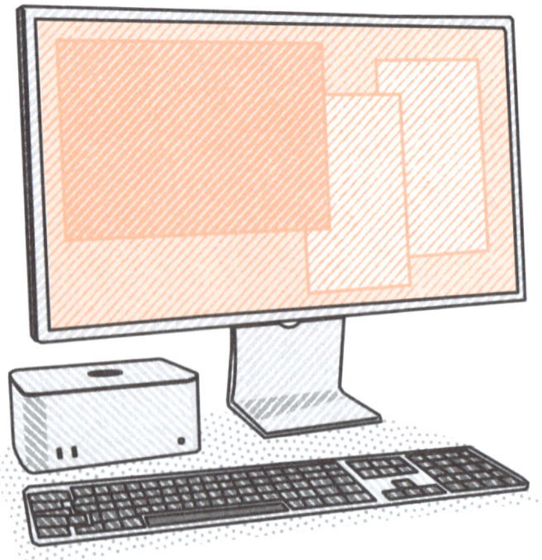

Laptops are portable, while desktops are more powerful

Hard drive(s)
With the size of image files these days, you won't last long using the memory on your computer, so you'll need external hard drives. We'll look at backup when we look at workflow, but you'll ideally need to keep three copies of each file for a secure backup system. So, you'll need multiple drives.

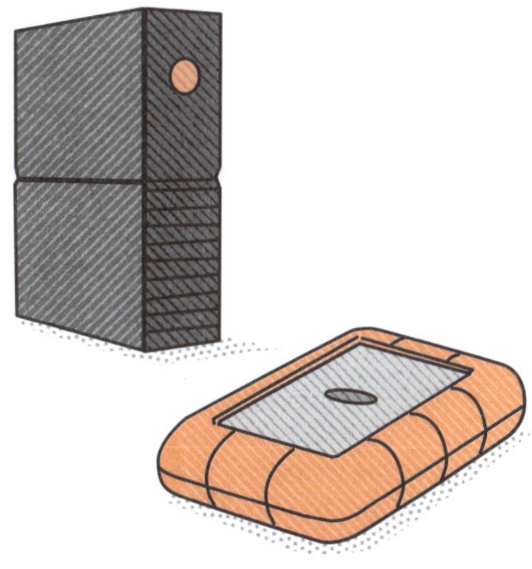

An additional portable hard drive can be useful for backing up when travelling

Software
There are many options. The first question is whether you want to subscribe or buy a perpetual licence. Subscription models are commonplace: the standard image-editing software, Adobe Lightroom and Photoshop, operate on a subscription model. Some people love it, others hate it. It probably makes sense if you're a serious, regular user – it's about the same cost as a movie-streaming service or a couple of cups of coffee monthly.

Accessories
Inevitably, you'll never have the right cable for this or the right adapter for that, so you'll no doubt end up with a box of odds and ends. It'll get bigger over time, as you'll never have the confidence to throw anything out in case it becomes useful one day. That's the story for many photographers.

Printer
A printer is not essential, and owning one opens a whole new can of worms, but if you do have an ambition to make prints, printing them yourself is an admirable route to take. Just don't be deluded into thinking that it'll save you any money over using a professional lab. It is, without doubt, rewarding to make a print and have complete control over the entire process.

Your ideal digital workflow...

1 – Shoot

The first stage in your digital workflow is, of course, taking a photo. This will get saved directly to the memory card in your camera. It is possible to circumnavigate this stage and tether your camera to a computer – this can be useful but is mainly used by pros in high-end studios.

2 – Import and name

Getting your files from the memory card to your computer or external hard drive can be done either directly from the camera (sometimes) or via a card reader.

3 – Back up

No matter how tempting it is to dive straight in and start getting creative, do your housekeeping first. The most important thing to do first is to create backups. Ideally, one image file should be saved in three locations: on two separate hard drives and one off-site location such as cloud storage or another drive somewhere else. Once your files are correctly backed up, you can format your memory card and use it again. Some image-editing software such as Adobe Lightroom will catalogue, rename and even keyword your files as you import them. Some photographers prefer to simply move the files over to specified folders, but naming and keywording is helpful in locating files later. Whatever naming convention and storage system you use, it is vitally important that you can find a file relatively easily in years to come.

4 – Process raw files

Processing your files and adding your creative twist is the fun bit. We'll look at this in a little more detail on the next page.

5 – Save as

Once you've finished your masterpiece, save a copy. There are a bunch of file formats to choose from, but only two are commonly used by photographers: JPEG and TIFF. See pages 54 and 181 for more on file formats.

6 – Print and/or share

And finally, you'll be ready to share your files, whether you make a print from your TIFF file or share online using a JPEG file. Voila!

DIGITAL WORKFLOW STEP-BY-STEP

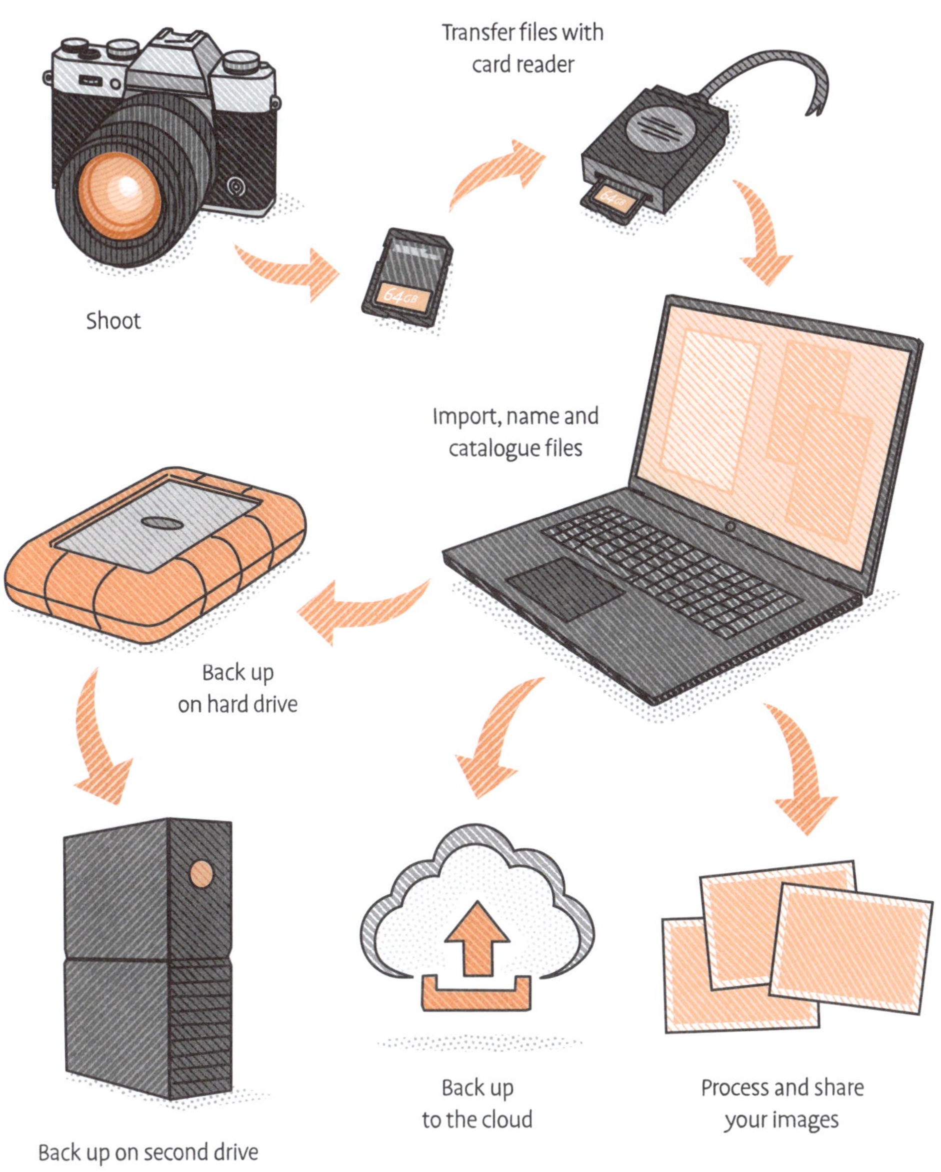

Raw processing is the fun and creative bit.

What do I do first?
Open your raw file in your chosen image-editing suite. Most software features a broadly similar set of controls. Getting the hang of the various sliders can take a while, and you'll no doubt find lots of valuable resources online. Most editors have some sort of 'tutor' mode that will prompt or tell you how to use a specific tool. It's only a matter of time before it becomes second nature.

So, the first thing you need to do is assess the image and ask yourself what you want it to 'say', and much like the creative shooting process, you can edit the image to those criteria.

Tones
A raw file straight from the camera can look a little 'flat' so tweaking the tones is the first port of call. You'll see sliders and controls for exposure, contrast, highlights, shadows, white points, dark points, and so on – experiment to get the look you want. Every image will be a little different. It can be tempting, especially at first, to think something looks amazing when a slider is cranked as far as it will go. In hindsight, this rooky error will make you cringe, so if you think something looks great at 100%, be safe and dial it back a bit.

Colour
You may need to tweak the colour too, and there will be sliders to alter the white balance along with the saturation and vibrance. Dig deeper and most software will allow you to target specific colours and tweak their vibrancy, hue and luminance.

Sharpening
There are tools to sharpen and reduce noise. Most images can benefit from sharpening but go easy, as the 'oversharpened' look is awful. And crucially, remember that sharpening is not something you use to try and salvage a blurred shot. It's there to enhance a well-focused shot for wherever it's intended to be seen, whether in print or online.

Cropping
Use the Crop tool to finesse your composition but be cautious about cropping too far, as you'll start compromising image quality. See this as a tool for making small adjustments such as straightening the horizon or slightly tweaking the edges of the frame.

Curves
Curves are just one of the many tools typically found in image-editing software. They might seem scary at first, but take the time to learn how to use them, and you'll unlock a whole world of creative potential.

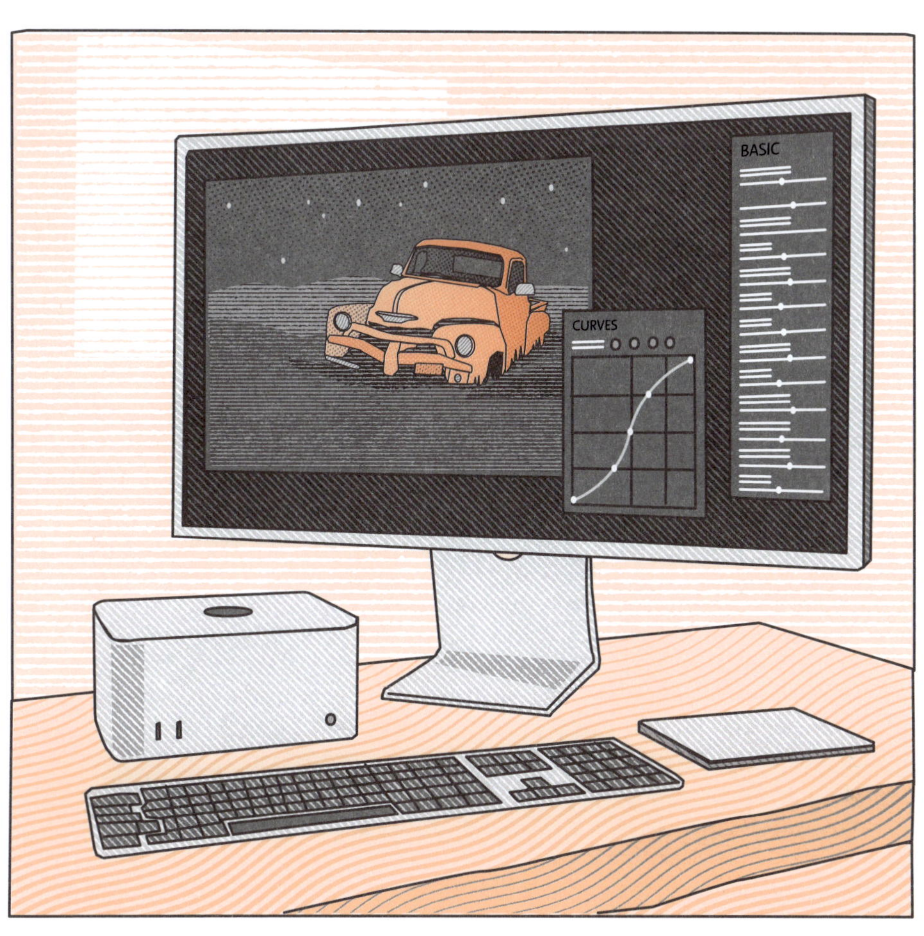

Learn to use the Curves tool for greater creative control

Workflow: sharing

Finally, but by no means least, there's the sharing of your images. After all you've done to express yourself creatively using the language of photography, you need to show the world!

Online

Build a dedicated website. There are many off-the-shelf portfolio sites specifically designed for photographers. Some are stunning and relatively inexpensive, and some even have features such as online stores so you can sell your work. How cool is that!

Social media

Instagram is the obvious choice for sharing images, and while it can be frustrating in some respects, it can also be a good place to showcase your work. Just don't let an appetite for likes and kudos ruin your experience. Sadly, social media can be fickle like that. On a positive note, it can be a great place to build a global community of like-minded folk.

Make a zine or book

Making a handmade book is a gratifying process, especially if you've created a coherent body of work. If you can't make a handmade book, there are plenty of online companies where you can upload your images, typically with templates allowing you to place and sequence your images and press print. Best of all, make a zine – what's not to love about the punk aesthetic of a low-fi magazine-style booklet of your images? Best of all, you don't need to be overly precious, as they're relatively inexpensive to make and there are a bunch of online companies that will print them for you.

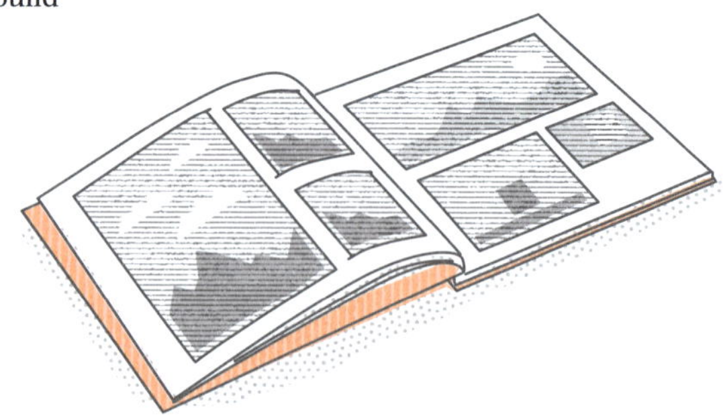

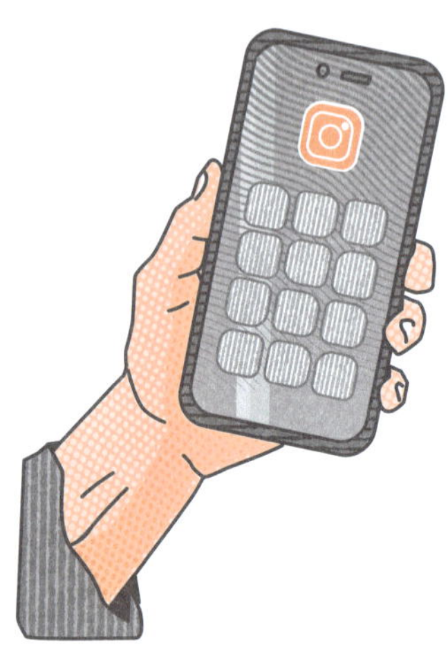

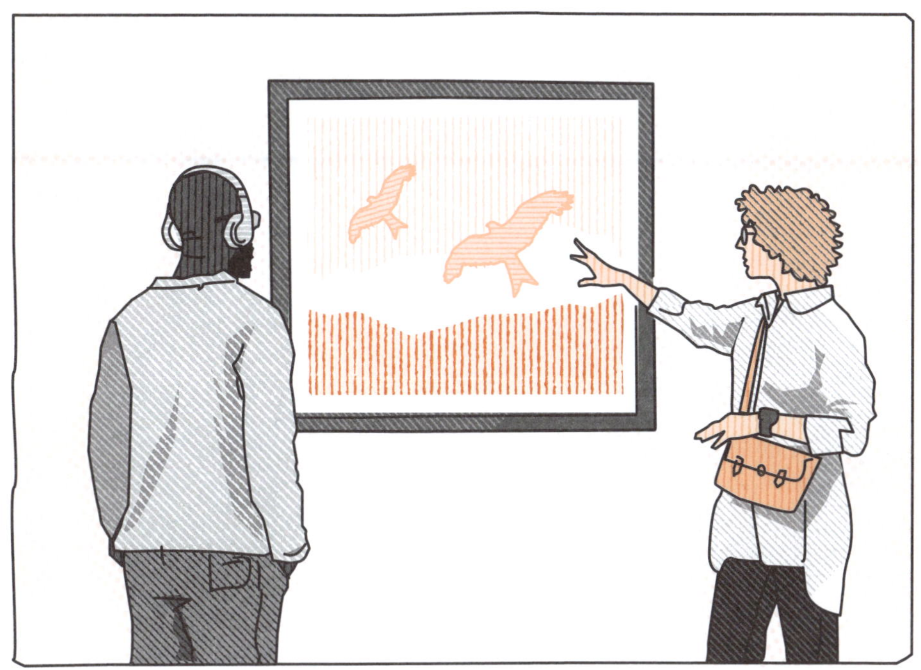

Have an exhibition

And for the grand finale, hold an exhibition. The only thing more rewarding than seeing one of your photographs framed and hanging on the wall is someone offering to purchase it and putting their money where their mouth is. Of course, money isn't the measure of creative success – that would be crass – but gosh, it isn't half a nice feeling.

Mindfulness and photography

There is a buzz around mindful photography nowadays – what is it?
'All the technique in the world doesn't compensate for the inability to notice,' said the great American photographer, Elliott Erwitt. And he's right! While this book is filled with lots of advice on various camera skills and techniques, none of these are a substitute for looking, seeing and noticing. Photography can be a great way to connect with the world around you.

How do I put this into practice?
The best place to start is simply slowing down. Take time to see and notice the world around you. Don't become obsessed with the sensational honeypot locations everyone else photographs. Rather, explore your local neighbourhood or even your domestic space and see what delights you can discover.

The Japanese photographer Rinko Kawauchi has said that she tries to tap into the child-like curiosity that lies dormant in so many people. In her beautiful, poetic work, she explores with a quiet and inquisitive eye the more mundane, often overlooked corners of everyday life with a transcendental reverence.

Also, tap into your other senses. For example, take some time to meditate on your sense of place if you find yourself in a new landscape location. Keep your camera in its bag for a while and use your other senses, such as smell, touch and sound, to build a picture of the place. Then, using the skills and techniques you've picked up in this book, set about translating those thoughts and feelings into a photograph.

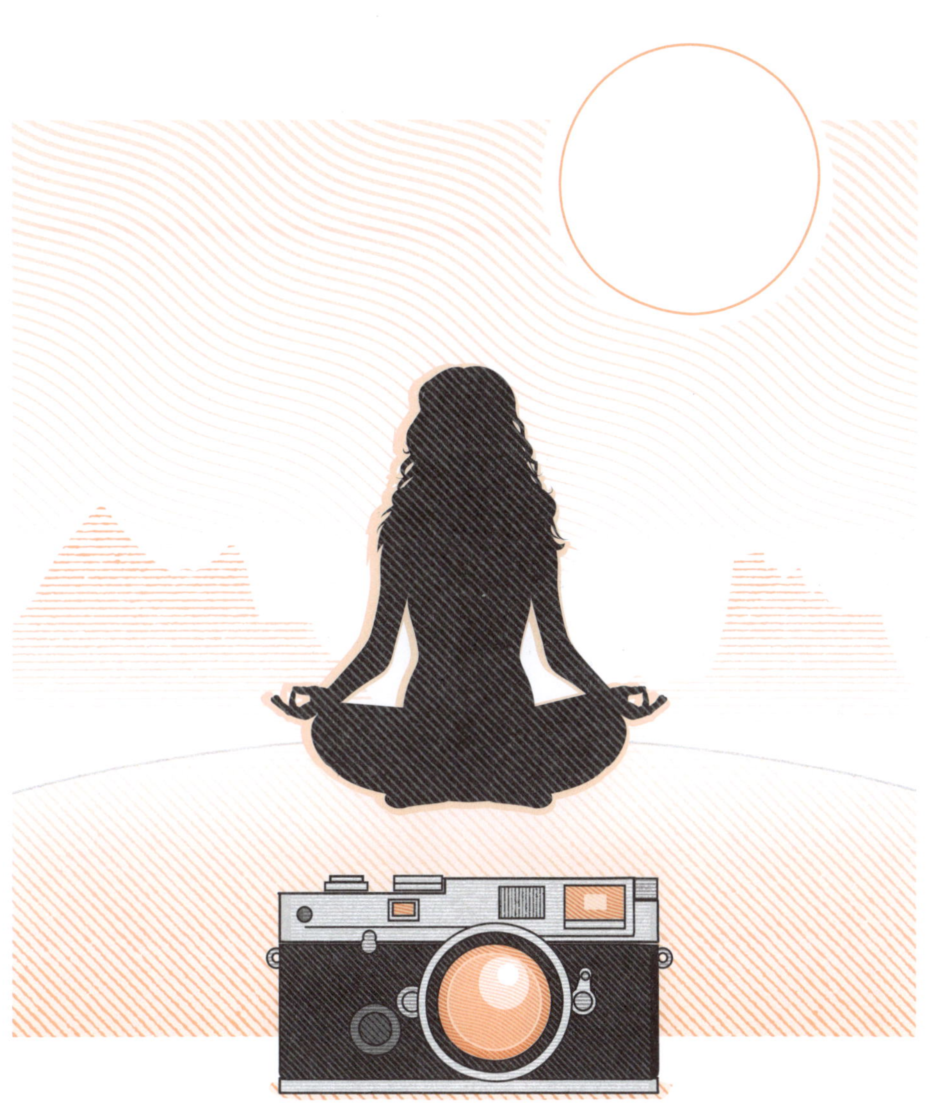

Post-production and mindfulness: Recap

The creative process doesn't stop when you press the shutter release. Once you're in the digital darkroom, there are many ways to enhance your photos, add cool effects or make subtle tweaks. Even a gentle shift in contrast or colour can change your story and help you realize your vision.

Five top tips

1 In most cases, shooting raw files, rather than JPEGs, will allow greater creative control and flexibility, although they will take up more space on your hard drive.

2 Always back your files up, ideally on three devices in multiple locations. At the very least, keep two copies of everything. Online, cloud-based storage can be a good option.

3 Adding cool effects and styles can be quite seductive when you first encounter image-editing software. However, overzealous use of sliders can look awful, so be restrained.

4 Use the language of photography to express how you feel and connect with the world. The art of looking, seeing and noticing will enrich your life. Have fun!

5 Share your work. Whether you hold an exhibition or simply post on social media, sharing your work can be a rewarding experience.

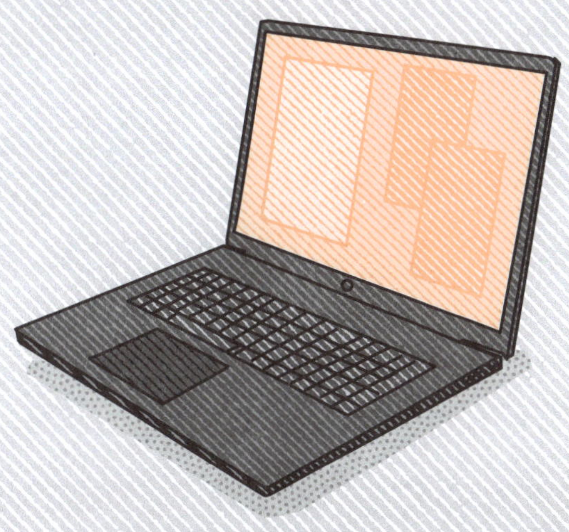

Further reading

This book will provide you with some of the core skills to help you get started with photography. You'll be able to experiment with new techniques and learn new skills. However, this is only the beginning of your incredible creative adventure. The real fun begins when you start flexing your creative muscles.

One of the best ways to do this is to look at the work of other photographers, talk to other creatives, read about art and photography, learn the history of photography and expand your knowledge. The following list of books, galleries and online sites will hopefully act as a springboard to your creative adventure.

If you can get to a gallery and see an exhibition in person, then I wholeheartedly encourage this. However, many galleries also have an online presence, so even if you cannot get to see a show in a distant land or city, the chances are you may be able to attend a talk or a virtual workshop – so keep an eye on them or sign up to their newsletters.

Books

You Will Be Able to Take Great Photos by The End of This Book by Benedict Brain
Naturally, as I wrote it, I'd suggest this book, but it is the perfect companion to this one and will help you develop your creative practice.

On Being a Photographer by Bill Jay and David Hurn
This book is a delightful conversation between two great photographic minds. The duo discuss everything from the best footwear to deeper photographic concepts in a jargon-free and accessible way.

Galleries & Online

The Photographers' Gallery
https://thephotographersgallery.org.uk/
Britain's premier photography gallery holds a series of world-class exhibitions. It also has a great café and store and hosts many talks and workshops in central London.

Magnum Photos
https://www.magnumphotos.com/
Magnum Photos is arguably the most prestigious agency in the world. Just browsing the work of its members is inspiration enough, but they also run workshops, talks, portfolio reviews, and much more.

International Center of Photography
https://www.icp.org/
Based in NYC, the International Centre of Photography features an impressive gallery space which showcases some amazing work. In addition, they also run courses, which are highly regarded and could be a great way to evolve your practice.

The Martin Parr Foundation
https://www.martinparrfoundation.org/
Magnum photographer Martin Parr founded this gallery and photography space in the heart of Bristol to support photographers who have made and continue to make work focused on Britain and Ireland.

Royal Photographic Society
https://rps.org/
With headquarters located next door, literally, to the Martin Parr Foundation (see above), The Royal Photographic Society offers a cool gallery space, lecture hall and an extensive programme of workshops, talks and events.

Magazines
Aperture Magazine
https://aperture.org/magazine/
My all-time favourite magazine. Founded by the great American photographer Minor White, this premium-quality magazine showcases some of the world's best photography. It's expensive but worth it.

Hotshoe Magazine
https://www.hotshoemagazine.com/
A beautifully produced showcase for contemporary photography.

Digital Camera Magazine
https://www.digitalcameraworld.com/
A consumer photography magazine full of popular techniques and kit-buying advice. Plus, you can also read my regular column, 'The Art of Seeing'!

Amateur Photograper Magazine
https://amateurphotographer.com/
Established in 1884, Amateur Photographer Magazine (AP) is the oldest photography weekly in the world. Aimed at enthusiasts, you'll get great kit reviews and features.

Extra terms

Contrast

Light and dark. Warm and cool. Hard and soft. These are all examples of the different kinds of contrasts available to photographers (and proponents of all creative mediums). Contrast describes opposites and is one of the major building blocks of strong composition. We can use it to create mood, enhance depth and direct the viewer's eye to a focal point. Contrast also goes hand in hand with light. For instance, images with bright highlights and dark shadows – think dramatic sunsets – are referred to as high-contrast images, while images with minimal tonal separation – think 'softer' images of newborn babies – are referred to as low-contrast images.

Crop factor

A digital camera's crop factor describes the difference in size between its sensor and the 35mm film format (yep, classic analogue technology is still relevant in the 21st century). For instance, full-frame sensors are the same size (36x24mm) and so have a crop factor of 1x. APS-C sensors (23.6x15.6mm or 22.2x14.8mm) are smaller and have a crop factor of 1.5x or 1.6x. Micro Four Thirds sensors (17.3x13mm) are smaller still and have a crop factor of 2x. To find a lens's effective focal length – the focal length needed to produce the same angle of view as a 35mm camera – when using anything other than a full-frame camera, multiply the stated focal length by the sensor's crop factor.

Exposure

We've looked at the exposure triangle in detail (see page 40), and knowing how shutter speed, aperture and ISO relate is essential for anyone wanting to shoot in manual or semi-automatic modes, but 'exposure' is a multi-purpose word that crops up in photographic parlance in other ways. For example, it's often used to refer to photos themselves in the same way that you'd use picture, image or shot, as in 'This exposure of Marilyn Monroe was truly iconic', and also to describe a shutter cycle i.e., long exposure or multiple exposure.

Field of view

Not to be confused with depth of field or angle of view, this technical-sounding term simply refers to the maximum amount of a scene – the 'observable' area – that can be seen through the viewfinder or LCD screen at any given moment. Field of view is expressed in degrees and is influenced by focal length, sensor size and the distance between sensor and subject. Wide-angle lenses have a broad field of view while telephoto lenses have a narrow field of view. In other words, you'll be able to see a lot more of a scene through a wide-angle lens than you would through a telephoto lens.

File formats

Every nugget of digital information is encoded and stored in a file of some sort. Common files we might use professionally include DOC, TXT and PDF. When it comes to image file formats, there's a sizeable list to choose from, but only a handful that are absolutely essential.

Probably the best known is JPEG, an acronym that stands for Joint Photographic Experts Group. JPEGs compress data, which means that a certain amount of detail is lost at the point of creation, but file sizes are small, and the format can be read by pretty much all devices.

Another popular image film format is TIFF, which stands for Tagged Image File Format. Unlike JPEGs, TIFFs are uncompressed and therefore high quality, but file sizes are large, and the format isn't as universally recognized.

Perhaps the most important image file type is raw, which simply refers to the capture of raw data and so isn't an acronym like JPEG or TIFF. This format stores all original data recorded at the point of capture, ready for manipulation and enhancement in editing software such as Adobe Photoshop. As a result, file sizes are huge, and raw files can't be viewed in their unprocessed form. You'll need bigger memory cards if shooting raw files, but the pros far outweigh the cons.

Focal length

Similar to field of view, focal length refers to how much of a scene your lens can see at any given moment. The difference is that focal length is a measurement of the distance between a lens's optical centre and the camera's sensor, which is given in millimetres and found on the barrel around a lens's front element. Lenses with focal lengths of 35mm or below are called wide-angle lenses, lenses with a focal length of 80mm or above are called telephoto lenses, and lenses with focal lengths between 35mm and 80mm are called 'standard' lenses, as they're roughly equivalent to the focal length of a human eye.

Metadata

Every time you press your camera's shutter, a whole heap of data is embedded in the image file. This 'metadata' can include the date and time of creation, author, file name, format and size, GPS location, dimensions and camera model and exposure settings. You can even add captions, keywords and copyright information to this metadata, which will both protect your images from online theft and make it a lot easier to locate certain images from your soon-to-be-extensive archives. Best of all, you don't even need fancy software to access metadata – just click on an image file, select 'Properties' or 'Get info' and hey presto. In a world in which billions of images are shared online every day, adding metadata should be an essential part of your workflow.

Monochrome
Monochrome literally means 'one colour', and so in the world of photography, the word refers to any image that contains varying tones, tints and shades of only one colour. Black and white is the obvious example, but blue and white (cyanotypes) and brown and white (sepia-toned prints) are other common combinations. Often shortened to 'mono', today the word is used interchangeably with black and white to describe any image containing shades of grey only, but there's a subtle yet important distinction. While all black-and-white images are monochrome by definition, not all monochrome images are black and white.

Noise
Noise appears as small dots or pixels in an image and is generated by higher ISO settings, low-light conditions and longer exposure times. Visually, it's roughly comparable to analogue film grain, and you'll often see the words noise and grain used interchangeably, but noise is generated by variations in the image signal rather than a chemical reaction. Noise is usually unwanted and there are various ways to reduce it, including using lower ISO settings, attaching your camera to a stable tripod and 'correcting' noise in editing software such as Adobe Photoshop.

Resolution
Camera resolution refers to the number of pixels located on a digital sensor and is calculated by multiplying the number of horizontal pixels by the number of vertical pixels. For example, the Sony A7 IV's sensor has an image size of 7,008x4,672 pixels, which gives a sensor resolution of 32,741,376 pixels or roughly 33 megapixels.

Image resolution refers to the number of pixels in an image and is an important factor to consider when viewing images on screen. This is measured in pixels per inch (PPI). Print resolution refers to the number of tiny droplets of ink that form an image and is measured in dots per inch (DPI).

Saturation
If you've ever experimented with the Saturation slider in Photoshop, you'll know that it relates to the intensity of a colour or image. Highly saturated colours tend to be 'shouty' and attention-grabbing, while less saturated colours tend to be quiet and more subdued. The human eye is very sensitive to saturation levels and perceived realism, so be careful when editing your photographs – pure colours are very rare in the real world due to the vagaries of natural light and it's easy to push saturation too far and create artificial-looking colours. It's worth noting that black-and-white (greyscale) images have no colour saturation.

Shutter types
There are two common types of shutters: focal plane and leaf. Most digital cameras feature the former. Situated just in front of the sensor, focal plane shutters consist of two curtains which open and close at high speed to allow a certain amount of light to reach the focal plane (the sensor). The mechanical nature of this system means that it is durable, reliable and allows for fast shutter speeds, usually up to 1/16,000sec, although flash sync speeds are often slower than a camera with a leaf shutter.

Leaf shutters are a more complex type that comprise a number of blades, or 'leaves', which overlap in a circular arrangement. When the shutter is pressed, these blades pivot from the centre outwards to allow light through. The leaves are typically located just behind the lens, which means they can be smaller, lighter and faster than focal plane shutters. Leaf shutters are typically found in medium-format cameras and are therefore more expensive, although flash sync speeds tend to be much faster.

Stops
Ever heard a photographer say they are 'stopping up' or 'stopping down' and wondered what they were talking about? A 'stop' is simply a measurement of light and is an integral term when talking about exposure and how the three sides of the exposure triangle relate to each other. Every time you double or halve the amount of light reaching the sensor, whether by changing the shutter speed, aperture or ISO, you're doing so by a stop.

For instance, if you increase the shutter speed from 1/60sec to 1/125sec, you're halving the amount of light by 1 stop. Similarly, if you change the aperture from f/5.6 to f/2.8, you're doubling the amount of light by 1 stop,

Tone/tonality
In the world of art and design (as opposed to writing or music), tone refers to how light or dark a colour appears and is determined by how light falls on an object. Colours can have an almost infinite number of tones, which are divided into three groups: light tones, mid-tones and dark tones. Particularly bright tones are called highlights and particularly dark tones are called shadows. It's a hugely important component of composition and content, as tone can be used to create the illusion of form and depth, and to suggest a particular atmosphere – photographs made up of mostly dark tones are known as 'low key' and can feel brooding and dramatic, whereas photographs made up of mostly light tones are known as 'high key' and can feel euphoric and lifting.

Index

R

S

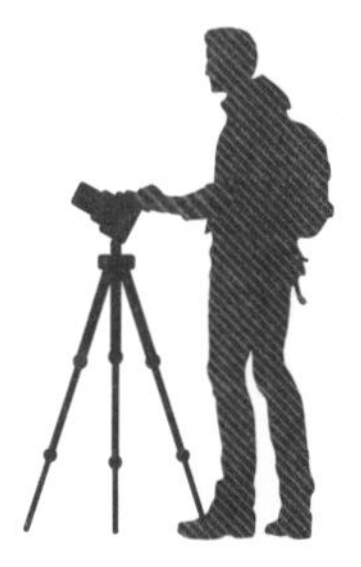

Picture credits

Illustrations by Chris Robinson, incorporating textures by Alex Gontar/Shutterstock, Irina Skokova/Shutterstock, and Kroljaa/iStock

Photographer silhouettes:
Mdjanntual/Adobe Stock and forgem/iStock

Page 3 background and repeats:
Vadym Ilchenko/iStock; 175 Wiktoria Matynia/Shutterstock

Acknowledgements

A special thanks to the fantastic creativity of Chris Robinson, who managed to translate my scrappy sketches into the fine collection of exquisite illustrations you see in this book. Thanks to Richard Collins for commissioning my second book! To Rachel Silverlight and Ben Hawkins for finessing and checking my words, and to Ben Gardiner for his super layout and vision!

Closer to home, my wonderful partner Kirstin and my son Rufus, for their support and patience as I tap and snap away. Hopefully, this book will be helpful to Rufus, who has just started GCSE photography!

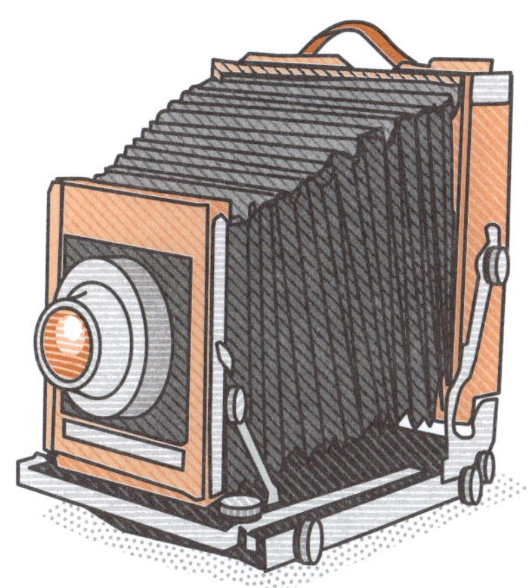

An Hachette UK Company
www.hachette.co.uk

First published in the UK in 2024 by ILEX,
an imprint of Octopus Publishing Group Ltd
Octopus Publishing Group
Carmelite House
50 Victoria Embankment
London, EC4Y 0DZ
www.octopusbooks.co.uk
www.octopusbooksusa.com

Distributed in the US by Hachette Book Group
1290 Avenue of the Americas, 4th & 5th Floors
New York, NY 10104

Distributed in Canada by Canadian Manda Group
664 Annette St, Toronto, Ontario, Canada M6S2C8

Publisher: Alison Starling
Commissioning Editor: Richard Collins
Managing Editor: Rachel Silverlight
Editorial Assistant: Stephanie Selçuk-Frank
Art Director: Ben Gardiner
Design: Chris Robinson
Senior Production Manager: Pete Hunt

ISBN 978-1-78157-929-9

A CIP catalogue record for this book
is available from the British Library

Printed and bound in China

10 9 8 7 6 5 4 3 2 1

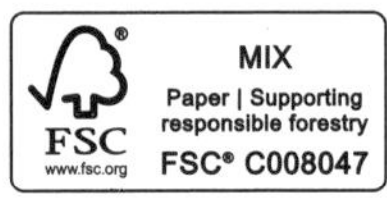